Praise for Dave's Complete Guide to Ministry

Dave Veerman has been passionate about junior high ministry for years. He writes from his expertise to provide a resource for youth workers everywhere. In this book you'll find not only the whys but also the how-tos for taking your ministry to the next level.

Denny Rydberg
President, Young Life

Those of us who are seasoned youth workers clearly understand that we must reach kids at an earlier age. In today's world, by the time they have made it to high school, they have been exposed to way too much. Dave Veerman gives strong rationale plus many practical how-tos that will help you reach blossoming teenagers.

Roger Cross
President, Youth for Christ/USA

The junior high years are no doubt the critical place where kids are making decisions that will last a lifetime. *Dave's Complete Guide to Junior High Ministry* is a youth ministry classic and a must read for all who care about kids. Dave Veerman is one of the world's premier experts on the subject and has written a most practical and helpful book.

Jim Burns
President, YouthBuilders

Hats off to all adults who are involved in ministry to junior high youth! And hats off to David Veerman for providing this excellent resource. As a volunteer youth leader for the past 18 years (with no retirement in sight), I appreciate the quality of this user-friendly book.

Kendra Smiley
Professional Speaker, Author of
Helping Your Kids Make Good Choices

Once again Dave Veerman is on target. With a concise gathering of information from his deep well of experience, Dave places in the hands of adults a super tool. From theory to creative application, what an engaging resource to help adults connect in what I feel is today's primary battle for a generation, the middle school years. Coming out of my discipline, I would say that Dave is right on key.

Freddie Langston
Recording Artist

According to the *Los Angeles Times*, the 14-year-old teenager is the most powerful person in Hollywood. That is why the entertainment industry markets their movies to the junior high and high school age groups. The church should be so concerned, and *Dave's Complete Guide to Junior High Ministry* is the book that every church leader needs to read and put into practice to prepare junior highers to survive the world's onslaught.

Having taught teenagers for 30 years—and often to junior high students—I only wish that I had read this book years ago. It has practical information, powerful insights and inspirational application to help deal with junior highers. This is an important book to reach children at a critical time in their development.

Ted Baehr
Chairman, The Christian Film and
Television Commission;
Publisher, *Movieguide*

A valuable, comprehensive guide for building the kind of junior high ministry that God can use to change lives. A must for every youth leader.

Paul Fleischmann
Executive Director, National
Network of Youth Ministries

Dave Veerman serves junior high youth workers the recipe they've been waiting for—a thoroughly Biblical ministry philosophy mixed with the practical wisdom of his decades of experience.

Dr. Kara Powell
Assistant Professor, Azusa Pacific
University, Azusa, CA; Assistant
Junior High Pastor, Lake Avenue
Church, Pasadena, California

With a 13-year-old living in my house, I am experiencing again the enormous value of ministry to junior highers. Dave Veerman lays the tracks for doing this with excellence in this dynamic guide to junior high ministry.

Barry St. Clair
President, Reach Out Youth
Solutions

This is a book that is thoughtful enough to give us the theory (and date) behind the practice, practical enough to take us beyond the theories, creative enough to stimulate some great how-to ideas, down-to-earth enough to speak to "real life junior high ministry," and genuine enough to remind us why working with junior high kids can be such a wild and (most of the time) fun adventure. This should be a helpful and hopeful resource for both professional and lay youth workers.

Duffy Robbins
Associate Professor of Youth
Ministry, Eastern College,
St. Davids, Pennsylvania

Dave's Complete Guide to Junior High Ministry has done for those working with junior high students what Dr. James Dobson has done for families. Dave Veerman has given us a Bible for junior high pastors, teachers, leaders and parents. The best I've seen in 22 years of speaking to teens!

Bill Sanders
Author; Teen and Parent
Motivational Speaker

Dave's
COMPLETE GUIDE TO
JUNIOR HIGH
MINISTRY

DAVE VEERMAN

Gospel Light

PUBLISHING STAFF
William T. Greig, Publisher
Dr. Elmer L. Towns, Senior Consulting Publisher
Pam Weston, Editor
Patti Pennington Virtue, Associate Editor
Jeff Kempton, Editorial Assistant
Kyle Duncan, Associate Publisher
Bayard Taylor, M.Div., Senior Editor, Biblical and Theological Issues
Dr. Gary S. Greig, Senior Advisor, Biblical and Theological Issues
Rob Williams, Cover Designer
Debi Thayer, Designer

ISBN 0-8307-2760-4
© 2001 Gospel Light, Ventura, CA 93006.
All rights reserved.
Printed in the U.S.A.

Library of Congress Cataloging-in-Publication Data
Veerman, David
    Dave's complete guide to junior high ministry/Dave Veerman.
        p. cm.
    Includes bibliographical references.
    ISBN 0-8307-2760-4
        1. Church work with youth. I. Title: Complete guide to junior high ministry. II.
    Title.
    BV4447.V385 2001-02-14
    259'.23—dc21   2001023083

Dedication

To the Veerman women—Gail, Kara and Dana—who give me much more love, understanding, support and encouragement than I deserve.

Contents

Foreword

When Jesus was 12 years old, He did what most all early adolescents do at that age—He asserted His independence by striking out on His own and worrying His parents half to death (see Luke 2:43-52). He knew He was ready to leave His childhood behind and to claim His identity as a young man—so off He went, forgetting perhaps to properly inform His earthly mom and dad. But the urge to explore the world of adulthood was just too exciting and irresistible. He was ready to ask questions, learn new ideas and listen to voices other than those in His small circle of influence back home in Nazareth. He was ready to find out more about Himself and His unique role in life. In short, He was ready to grow up.

In that sense, Jesus was no different from today's 12-year-olds. When He arrived at the Temple, He was fortunate to find a few adults who were willing to talk with Him and answer His questions. We are told that the teachers who spent time with Jesus that day were "amazed at his understanding" (v. 47). Even though He was what we would today call a preteen or junior high kid, they didn't shuttle Him off to the children's department or the Temple playground. A few verses later, we read that Jesus "grew in wisdom and stature, and in favor with God and men" (v. 52). He turned out to be a fine young man. And I have a feeling those teachers in the Temple contributed to that result. Because they took time for Jesus, they were rewarded by getting a nice mention in Luke's Gospel.

I'm glad they did. We who work with junior high students (sixth, seventh and eigth grades) need all the biblical support we can get for what we do. After all, it's not easy to convince people today that junior high ministry is important—perhaps the most important ministry of all. Despite what we know about this age group, it's still difficult to persuade the leadership of the Church to commit their best people and best resources to reach and teach early adolescents.

What do we know about this age group? First, we know that they are at life's most important transition. They are moving from childhood to adulthood. Contrary to popular belief, they are not becoming *teenagers* but *adults*. They are acquiring adult bodies, adult brains, adult skills and adult relationships. What they need are adult mentors who will help guide and direct them into adulthood in healthy and positive ways.

Second, we know that early adolescents are opening up to new ideas, new ways of thinking, new ways of behaving—perhaps more so than at any other time in their lives. They are ready to experience life, to experiment, to take risks. Today's advertising and marketing industry deliberately targets this age group, because they know how responsive these young people can be. Hook them while they're young and they'll be hooked for life.

Third, they are ready to make decisions—to take control of their lives, to commit themselves to whatever grabs their attention and allegiance. They are ready to start making choices, which of course many of them do. It's no wonder so much of high school ministry is rehabilitation work. Young people today are making serious life-changing decisions (many of them, irrevocable) before they ever get to high school.

Add all that to the fact that today's early adolescents are uniquely neglected, lacking in the kind of adult supervision and guidance that they need at this critical juncture of life, and it's easy to see that we have a problem. We are losing a lot of kids before they ever have a chance to discover who Jesus is or what God wants for their lives. They come to their Father's house and find nobody home.

When Jesus taught "whatever you did for one of the least of these . . . you did for me" (Matt. 25:40), He may very well have been thinking about junior highers. He may have been thinking about *Himself*—that day when He was only 12, when He strolled onto the Temple grounds a bit awestruck and no doubt very afraid. He may have remembered a nameless person who graciously escorted Him into the company of some teachers who were willing to share their wisdom and knowledge with Him. He may have remembered that when He said "whoever welcomes this little child in my name welcomes me" (Luke 9:48).

My friend and colleague Dave Veerman is one of those rare adults who loves junior highers and has always been willing to spend time with them. For more than 30 years, he has not only been one of the nation's most creative junior high workers but also one of the nation's best trainers and equippers of junior high workers. His leadership and influence over the years in Youth For Christ/USA has especially been significant, as he has written and developed much of YFC's Campus Life JV, a program that has been widely used to reach and disciple thousands of junior high students.

Dave has also authored dozens of books for youth workers, parents and teens, but hardly any of them is more important than the one you now hold in your hands. That's why it was recently revised and updated to be even more helpful to adults who want to be effective with today's kids. It's not a curriculum or canned program but a guidebook to help you better understand junior high and middle school students and to give you the tools to meet their needs both developmentally and spiritually. *Read it and catch the vision.*

—Wayne Rice
Cofounder, Youth Specialties
Director, Understanding Your Teenager seminars
Author, *Junior High Ministry* and *Enjoy Your Middle Schooler*

Acknowledgments

Special thanks to the following youth ministry experts who took time to read the manuscript and offer invaluable guidance and suggestions:

Dr. Bruce B. Barton, president of The Livingstone Corporation (Carol Stream, Illinois)

Dr. Richard Dunn, pastor of Leadership Formation, Fellowship Church (Knoxville, Tennessee)

Dr. James Galvin, president of James C. Galvin & Associates, Inc. (Winfield, Illinois)

Greg Johnson, former editor of *Breakaway Magazine* (Focus on the Family)

The Rev. Tim Kirk, senior pastor of Christ Community Church (Carmel, Indiana)

Laura Laffoon, vice president, Communication Resources (Alma, Michigan)

Greg Lafferty, teaching pastor, Christ Community Church (St. Charles, Illinois)

Scott Pederson, Student Ministries, Willow Creek Community Church (South Barrington, Illinois)

Len Woods, pastor of Community Life, Christ Community Church (Ruston, Louisiana)

Chapter One

"Junior Highers? You've Got to Be Kidding!"

"You've got to be kidding!" she almost shouted back to me in the church foyer. You would have thought that I had pressured her for a large donation to the building fund, urged her to preach or inquired about a personal matter. But I had only asked if she would consider helping teach the junior high Sunday School class.

I shouldn't have been surprised. Even professional youth workers cringe when they hear the words "junior highers." The mental image is the Tasmanian Devil of Bugs Bunny cartoons—a whirling tornado of unlimited energy, boundless curiosity and ravenous appetite, devastating everything and everybody in its path.

This caricature arises from our memories of junior high; it is further reinforced by our observations of kids at church or in the neighborhood; it is finally confirmed by our own children as they enter adolescence.

Ask a group of adults what they remember about junior high (sixth, seventh and eighth grades), and you'll get an earful. Painful memories are brought to the fore—struggles with peers, popularity, pimples and puberty. Others remember physical frustrations as they coped with growth or the lack of it—cherubic boys yearning to be bigger and taller, and gangly girls wishing they could shrink.

Our Recollections

"Quiet!" With his face contorted in anger, Mr. Jackson whirled from the blackboard and slammed his fist on the desk. A momentary hush fell over the classroom, but the whispers, notes and flying objects resumed as soon as he turned back to the board.

We tormented that poor algebra teacher all year. He could not control us, and we knew it. In fact, during one class period, he said "Quiet!" 63 times. I know; we counted—out loud.

That's one of my vivid junior high memories.

Jean, 45, recalled the day she lowered a friend out of the school window, so she could run to the store for candy.

Frank, 36, remembered fighting constantly to prove how tough he was.

Betsy, 40, recalled getting her period and the embarrassment of pimples.

 What does repression have to do with junior high ministry? Simply this: psychologists tell us that some of life's most painful experiences occur during early adolescence—while we are junior highers. So we repress our early adolescence. We block it from memory. Once we leave those adolescent years behind, we forget them. —Wayne Rice, *Junior High Ministry* [1]

I also remember going from 140 to 170 pounds in one year, throwing an egg at a car to be accepted by the popular kids in my new neighborhood and trying desperately to impress certain girls.

The stories could go on and on. No wonder adults are wary of getting involved with this age group.

Our Responses

Remembering vividly the painful moments of their junior high years, adults respond in various ways to the real, live junior highers in their world.

Harangue

Some adults react to junior highers with judgment and criticism. Seeing the eighth-grade girls write and pass notes during the worship service or seeing the sixth-grade boys run through the sanctuary afterward, they shake their heads and criticize.

"I can see from their faces that Beth and Kara really want to be here," a young father commented sarcastically to my wife one Sunday.

Your day is coming, she answered silently as she thought of his seven-year-old son.

Others complain to parents and principals and write vitriolic letters about neighborhood mischief. They also point judgmental fingers and comment about today's kids to anyone who will listen.

It's easy to criticize and complain because early adolescents always seem to be getting into trouble, acting silly or displaying bad attitudes. They are visible targets.

Hide (and Don't Seek)

Some adults respond to junior highers by ignoring them, acting as though they don't exist. Babies are "darling" and are smothered with "cootchy-coos" and kisses. Toddlers and preschoolers look and sound so cute and are complimented on their physical progress. Even grade school children receive loads of attention from doting grandparents, church members, neighbors and family friends. But around sixth grade, children become invisible. Adults often avoid them, acting as though they aren't there.

> Most people feel totally unequipped to work with kids in the age group where the maturity levels span the spectrum between Transformers and Trojans. All it really takes, however, is someone who will *love them* in the midst of all their diversity and someone who will look at the big picture and wait for God to bear fruit in his time, not theirs. —Greg Johnson, former editor of *Breakaway* (Focus on the Family's magazine for teenage boys)

Mark Twain is reported to have humorously recommended to put children in barrels, feed them through the knotholes and then, when they reach adolescence, close up the holes!

Many people respond that way—avoiding, ignoring, sealing off junior highers—virtually hiding and pretending that they don't exist. That's why the junior high age group is one of the most neglected in the Church. There are programs for almost everyone else, from babies to senior citizens. Singles, young couples, parents and older adults have a smorgasbord of activities from which to choose. And when a youth director arrives, his or her commission is usually to work with the high schoolers (and, perhaps, advise the junior high sponsors).

Those who *hide* want to leapfrog over the junior high years. (By the way, when these kids are ignored, they tend to act up even more, doing almost anything to be noticed.)

Hope

This reaction is similar to hiding but relates more to parents. Nothing strikes fear into a parent's heart more than having his or her oldest child about to enter junior high school (I'll discuss this more in chapter 4).

These parents have read about teenagers, have heard stories and are scared to death.

Often they talk as though early adolescence is just another stage through which their children must pass, like thumb sucking or the terrible twos, and they hope their kids will survive.

These parents tend to withdraw, treating older children with benign neglect while hoping for the best.

Unfortunately, this reaction can blind parents to their young teens' problems and related symptoms. Junior highers who experiment with drugs, alcohol or sex are not experts at camouflaging their actions. Mom and Dad are often shocked when the habits come to light, because they haven't seen the obvious signs.

- Ken brags about how he can sneak off to do whatever he wants.
- Celeste laughs about how her mom believes anything she tells her.
- Keri is a model child at home and at church, but she is a terror at school.

Simply hoping for the best is foolish and irresponsible and, in fact, will only make a challenging time even more difficult.

Hire

Another response to the presence of junior highers at church or in our families is to employ a professional youth worker to deal with them (few churches do this). Aware of the problems and pressures of early adolescence, concerned adults believe that the only answer is to hire someone who has been specially trained to work with this difficult age group. The profile for the youth worker usually includes the following: young, good-looking, athletic, musical, funny, creative, spiritual, intelligent, firm, married and willing to work for peanuts—a combination of Michael Jordan, Mother Teresa, Steven Spielberg, Rebecca St. James and Ray Romano.

This person is expected to attract, entertain, teach, discipline and lead young people to Christ and spiritual maturity—a most unrealistic task.

 Never mind the youth director's philosophy of ministry, stated objectives, creative programming or well-intentioned efforts. *When evaluating their church's youth group, the bottom line for most parents is "Does my child enjoy it?"* —Clayton Baumann, veteran youth worker with Florida Youth For Christ, Palm Beach County

On the positive side, adults who respond by hiring help are aware of and very sensitive to the needs of this age group. They will form a powerful lobbying influence within the church, forcing church leaders to remember early adolescents when setting the budget or adding staff.

The problem with this response, however, is that it assumes a person can be found who meets the ideal profile and that one person will be able to minister to all the kids in the group. In reality, every child is different and represents a unique set of challenges and opportunities. Unrealistic expectations for those we hire usually result in discouragement, disappointment or disillusionment.

Another problem with this response is that it pushes the responsibility onto other people, assuming that they are more qualified and will be more effective than we could be. Actually, it is a common North American reaction to think that we can hire a specialist to cover any situation or that we can throw money at a problem to solve it while we sit and watch. Professionals can offer great expertise, and money certainly helps, but human beings and their problems are more complex than any simple solution.

Help

The final response is "What can I do to help?" Obviously this is my punch line—the response I was getting to and the one I endorse.

Adults who care about the junior high children in their churches, families or neighborhoods can have a significant ministry with these young people in a variety of ways. Instead of criticizing or avoiding them or expecting someone else to do everything, they can do the following:

- **Pray** for the early adolescents they know, for their parents and for those who are ministering to them.
- **Affirm** the junior highers they know, greeting them by name and offering compliments whenever possible.
- **Assist** those who carry the main ministry load by driving, phoning, collecting props for meetings and doing other necessary tasks.
- **Reach out** directly to young people by teaching a Sunday School class, counseling at a camp or retreat, sponsoring a youth group, leading a small group or spending time with certain junior highers.
- **Lead** by organizing a junior high ministry team at church, a parents' council, a neighborhood youth group, and so forth, and by being an advocate for junior high ministry.

The importance of church life in the spiritual development of people cannot be overestimated—nor should it be minimized. But we also know that teenagers are still in a formative stage spiritually. They attend churches for a variety of reasons—and those experiences will shape their desires and expectations regarding church life as they age. —George Barna, *Third Millennium Teens* [2]

Junior high ministry is important. It is also demanding. If you do it, you will be stretched like never before. You will also lose your mind. (How do you think I lost mine?) —Len Woods, pastor of Community Life at Christ Community Church, Ruston, Louisiana

Think again about your own junior high years. What adults played a significant, positive role in your life? And what did they *do* that you still remember today? You can be that kind of person for the early adolescents around you.

Think It Through

1. What kind of person were you in junior high (sixth, seventh and eighth grades)?

2. Describe a negative experience from those years.

3. Describe a positive experience from those years.

4. List the names of the early adolescents you know.

5. Which word best describes your response to this age group (circle one): harangue, hide, hope, hire, help. Explain.

6. In what ways would you like to help minister to junior highers in your world?

Chapter Two

At the Crossroads

- With bright eyes shining, Traci could hardly wait for third grade to begin. Miss Kramer made learning an exciting adventure (she was "the best teacher in the world!"), text-books opened a new world and all of Traci's friends were with her in school. As the elementary years passed, Traci didn't even mind doing homework, although she needed occasional prodding from her mom and dad. She was a model daughter and student. That was four years ago. Today, Traci is into hard rock, she has painted her room black and her hair blue, and she hangs out with troubled kids at school. Arguing constantly with her parents, Traci has thought and talked about running away.

- He seemed shy, but when you got to know Jeff, you discovered a pleasant personality and a great sense of humor. Jeff was a good student, especially in fourth grade when he won awards in science and English. He's in eighth grade now—just barely, after taking math again in summer school.

- King of the Playground was Michael's nickname. He could run faster, jump higher and throw a ball farther than anyone else in school, even the boys in the next grade. Michael looked older, and he walked the halls with a self-assured confidence. Everyone knew he was destined for stardom. But today, Michael just hangs around the playgrounds. He should be a junior in high school, but he dropped out—after being suspended several times for fighting during the last few years.

What made the difference in each of these young lives? What did they have in common? What changed Traci, Jeff and Michael from optimistic, happy and fun-loving children into sullen and rebellious teenagers? The answer? Their junior high experience.

These are the crossroad years where young people choose paths that can change their lives. These years are crucial for physical, emotional, moral, mental, social and spiritual development. In 1989, a *Time* magazine article stated:

Television calls them the wonder years, but for millions of youths between the ages of 10 and 15, the years of early adolescence are anything but wonderful. No longer children, not quite adults, they are bombarded by dizzying physical changes, reeling emotions, and raging hormones. Today's youngsters, however, face problems far more formidable than acne or gangly limbs.

Drinking, drug abuse, sexually transmitted diseases, and teenage pregnancy, once the province of high schools, have drifted into the lower grades.[1]

Today the situation is even more critical.

Events that have been reported in the world of children and adolescents in the last years can make one feel numb and discouraged. We hear of students killing or attempting to kill one another, there are reports of frequent suicidal responses and suicide pacts among teens, and rampant sexual activity is found in younger and younger children. It appears that the world of children and adolescents is out of control.[2]

The pressures and problems that we faced in college or high school are now the struggles of much younger kids. It is a generation at risk. Let's take a closer look at what junior highers are facing.

You can see the lights going out. It seems to happen somewhere in junior high. A child goes in soft and comes out hard. He enters laughing and innocent . . . he leaves unsmiling and jaded. The eclipse shouldn't come so fast, so soon. But it does.

The moral crossroads that used to come in college or high school have moved to junior high, to middle school. By eighth grade, a young person will probably have to decide about his first drink, his first drugs, and his first sexual experience. One out of five will have sex *before* they enter high school.
—Ron Hutchcraft, president of Ron Hutchcraft Ministries, Harrison, Arkansas

They Are Rushed

As we ate dinner one October afternoon, my second grader laughed and said, "She was probably on drugs." It was just a passing comment—she didn't mean anything by it, but I almost fell out of my chair. During *my* high school years, we hardly ever heard of drugs. They may have been used by people in crime areas of big cities far away but not in our town or by anyone we knew. But my grade school daughter had just made a casual reference to drugs as a natural part of conversation.

Today, grade schoolers know all about drugs and why they shouldn't take them—and who does. They know about child abuse, AIDS and dangerous strangers. They see warnings on TV, hear them on the radio, read them in magazines and hear them in the classroom. In this age of information, especially with the growth of the Internet, they are barraged with news reports, warnings, educational programs and special bulletins.

A new survey by Grunwald Associates indicates that more than 70 percent of all U.S. teenagers are regularly surfing the Internet. In all, more than 25 million youngsters aged 2-17 are on-line, three times the number pegged in a 1997 survey. Projections call for almost 44 million children on the Internet by 2005, with the primary access locale shifting from home to school sometime in 2003 as classroom wiring initiatives kick in. —Grunwald Associates, "Children, Families, and the Internet 2000"[3]

Don't get me wrong. I think we should put pictures of missing kids on milk cartons and trucks, educate children about the bad guys out there and participate in Neighborhood Watch. These are the helpful, positive benefits of high-tech communication. But a negative result is the loss of innocence for children. Even before they can talk, they learn that the world is a frightening and dangerous place in which to live. The bogeyman is real.

Add to these helpful communiqués the usual television fare of sex and violence, the lurid lyrics of popular music and the twisted values of many videos and movies, and you see the massive assault on young hearts and minds.

 Adolescence is not a mistake—it is a perfection! It is an exact and perfect stage of growth and development that is the period of changing from child to adult. The very features of adolescence that are so frustrating to parents and adolescents themselves—adolescent illusions of greatness, the adolescent preoccupation with freedom and independence—these features are the way they are because the Great Creator, in his infinite wisdom and unlimited power, has designed adolescence as an ideal, final preparation for adulthood.
—Dr. Jim Geddes, *You Can Enjoy Your Teen*[4]

Kids are also rushed by parents and the educational system. There are music lessons, classes for gifted students, sports teams and camps for every age. For many families, school and play have become serious business.

Dealing with adult problems at their tender age and being pushed to accelerate their pace of learning, our children are forced to grow up too fast.

 Adolescence is a transitional state; you are neither child nor adult. Everything begins to happen at once. You look in the mirror and see your body changing. The hormonal changes lead to feelings and drives you've never had before; members of the opposite sex become more attractive to you. Friendships and family relationships change. Emotional changes cause you to feel more but understand less. You start to think in new and different ways. You even begin to question things that you always thought were true. Adolescence is a period full of demands and changes.
—Walt Mueller, *Understanding Today's Youth Culture* [5]

They Are Pressured and Tempted

Children today also face pressures unheard of in previous generations. North America is in the throes of a drug and alcohol epidemic, and substance abusers are younger and younger. A 1983 study by the Search Institute of Minneapolis reported that 26 percent of high school seniors had their first experience with alcohol in the seventh grade or earlier. In sharp contrast, 56 percent of eighth graders reported having their first drink of alcohol in the seventh grade or earlier. This is a major difference, with a rate of seventh-grade or earlier use by eighth graders double that of high school seniors.[6] A more recent study by the Parent's Resource Institute for Drug Education found that in 1997, monthly drug use among 11- to 14-year-olds increased by 5 percent. Among girls, 31 percent of new users of alcohol and 24 percent of new users of marijuana are between the ages of 10 and 14—up from 7 and 5 percent in the 1960s.[7]

In a study of students from Minnesota and Colorado, Search Institute also found that:

- nearly all eighth graders had some experience with alcohol;
- one out of three had used an illicit drug;
- one out of four had used alcohol 20 or more times;
- one out of six had had more than five drinks in the two weeks preceding the survey.

Furthermore, after surveying 8,000 fifth- through ninth-grade American students who indicated that they were active in a church, parish or synagogue, Search Institute reported that:

- one out of four fifth and sixth graders had used alcohol in the last 12 months; and
- one out of ten sixth graders had gotten drunk at least once in the last year.[8]

Young people also feel pressure to be sexually active. Consider the typical plots for many television shows; broken marriages, adultery and assorted affairs are assumed to be a natural part of life. Movies and videos are even worse, displaying scenes in PG or PG-13 films that would have been considered pornography just a few years ago.

MTV and other music video outlets also play a major role in influencing our children. Since the '50s, rock 'n' roll has been a dominant force in youth culture. Before MTV, only a handful of young people on any high school or junior high campus became devoted followers of rock stars. They could buy records, hear songs on the radio, watch an occasional appearance on television and perhaps attend a concert of their favorite artist. Today, however, musicians will perform in our homes at the push of a button, allowing us to see their antics and hear their messages over and over. And rock stars seem to try to outdo each other in sexual explicitness, obscenities and outrageousness.

In addition, many of the rock radio stations feature disc jockeys who major in dirty talk and double meanings. It's called trash radio, and it's on the rise. Young people love music and are attracted by this kind of shock humor—and they are influenced by what they hear.

This tremendous emphasis on sex is having an effect. According to a study by the Allan Guttmacher Institute, 7 million boys and 5 million girls between the ages of 13 and 19 are sexually active. Each year, 1.1 million teenage girls become pregnant; 30,000 of these girls are under the age of 15.[9] According to the National Center on Addiction and Substance Abuse at Columbia University, in 1972, less than 5 percent of 15-year-old girls and just 20 percent of 15-year-old boys had engaged in sexual intercourse. In 1997, however, 38 percent of 15-year-old girls and 45 percent of 15-year-old boys had engaged in sexual intercourse.[10] Studies by Search Institute indicate that 15 percent of seventh graders and 18 percent of eighth graders will have sexual intercourse one or more times this year.[11] And Kay S. Hymowitz reports that

even middle schoolers can be blasé these days. . . . They lie about being virgins. According to Michael Cohen, a research psychologist and principal of Arc Consulting, nine-and ten-year-old girls, whose counterparts in the past always looked forward to becoming teenagers, now say they are afraid.[12]

Because young people see and hear so much about drinking, drugs and sex, they tend to see those activities as normal and are more apt to give in. But the greatest pressure comes from peers. Wanting to be accepted and to be more adultlike, early adolescents are quite vulnerable to the well-worn line "Everybody's doing it." No one wants to be outside of the crowd.

They Are Growing

Early adolescence marks a time of tremendous growth for our children, in just about every area of life.

Physical Growth

The junior high years bring the most obvious area of growth, rapid physical development. This development happens earlier for girls than for boys. And there is usually a growth spurt. (As I mentioned earlier, I gained 30 pounds in one year!) This growth produces enormous appetites, a lack of coordination, awkwardness, self-consciousness and alternating periods of energy and fatigue. And these physical changes can wreak havoc with a young person's self-concept.

The junior high years also mark a growth in sexual awareness. Puberty usually begins around the age of 10 for girls and 11 for boys. Sex organs develop, voices change, pubic hair appears, pimples pop out and hormones rampage. Usually this is when boys begin to masturbate, leading to feelings of confusion and guilt. A new awareness of the opposite sex and an obsession with one's own body develops. Boys begin to wonder if they'll ever get taller, girls wonder if they'll every stop growing, and both spend hours in front of the mirror.

Girls go through puberty like Grant took Richmond, alternating screaming laughter with screaming hysteria, interspersed with sullen silences when "she" (meaning me, her mother) comes into the room. Girls of 13 are already conscious of the fact that they have a figure and that it, like a really good lawn, will need life-long maintenance. They "diet" by skipping dinner and munch on a lettuce leaf while the family gorges. They balance this with telling sympathetic friends over after-school pizza or French fries that "she" never serves anything but starches. —Janet Cool, "Nearing Adulthood, or: Why You'd Hate to be 13 Again"[13]

Intellectual Growth

Jean Piaget (1896-1980), an eminent Swiss psychologist famous for his studies of the thought processes of children, identified four stages of a child's cognitive development. Children (ages 7 to 11) in stage 3, the concrete operations stage, don't think abstractly or conceptually. Instead, they think more in terms of the concrete and cause and effect. Children (11 and up) in stage 4, the formal operations stage, begin to use logic and to think in terms of concepts and abstract ideas. Junior highers are in transition mentally, beginning to think and learn abstractly.

School can be an exhilarating or discouraging experience as students are presented with an array of facts and concepts. During these years, certain students may jump ahead, discovering the world of ideas, opening their imaginations and understanding the potential results of their choices and actions. But others may be left behind, ignored by teachers who gravitate toward the brighter students.

The educational process for many young people is like explaining how to operate a computer to a jungle tribesman. He may hear what you are saying, memorize the parts and even understand how the machine works, but he will still be confused because the whole discussion is out of his context.

In the same way, early adolescents don't have the context of life experience and perspective to be able to understand fully all that they are being taught.

As an assignment for a class I was teaching at Wheaton College in suburban Chicago, two female students from Indiana and Wisconsin interviewed two 12-year-old girls at the mall. These junior high girls shared freely about their boyfriends, sex and their thoughts of marriage. Suddenly one of the girls turned to my student and said, "Do they have television in Wisconsin?" This girl knew all about sex and was even talking about marriage, but she knew very little about life.

> Growing up today feels tougher than ever. While the cases may be extreme, the tragedies at Columbine High School last spring, and just recently at the National Zoo, are chilling reminders of the stress, alienation, and violence that can overwhelm a troubled teen. . . . The time between childhood and adulthood is pivotal. The choices teens make, the values they adopt now can determine whether they become happy and productive citizens. Together we can help them to make choices that are good for them, and for all of us. —Hillary Rodham Clinton, U.S. Senator-elect, New York[14]

In my junior high Sunday School class we were discussing Jesus' confrontation with the Gerasene demoniac—the Bible describes him as being a wild man, with broken chains hanging off his arms because "no one was stronge enough to subdue him" (Mark 5:4). As I described what must have been a frightening scene to the disciples, one of the boys exclaimed, "Why didn't they shoot him?" This young man had not been able to put the story into its historical context. Early adolescence is definitely a time of intellectual transition and growth.

The nation's middle and junior high schools—encompassing grades 6 through 9—play a potentially crucial role in shaping the future of young adolescents. Yet these institutions have largely been left out of a flurry of educational reforms that have focused on U.S. elementary and secondary schools over the past several years. —Susan Tifft, *Time* [15]

Social Growth

Junior highers are also growing and changing socially. In elementary school, my best friend lived next door, and we did everything together. But when I went to junior high school (grades seven to nine), we drifted apart, mainly because he was held back to repeat sixth grade.

My experience is typical for the age. During elementary school, a child's friends can be found in the neighborhood, because his or her mobility is limited and the school is probably nearby. In junior high, however, these friendships begin to change, centering more on common interests and activities.

Early adolescents can seem obsessed with their friends, forming tight cliques, writing copious notes and talking incessantly on the phone. Friends are important, because fragile egos need acceptance, affirmation and a place to belong. And while young people feel almost desperate to be part of a group, they can be very cruel to those who are different or outside their circle of friends. I've heard kids gang up on an individual and mock him unmercifully. It's as though they have to protect themselves by lashing out at others. Some people never quite recover from those verbal beatings, carrying scars in their psyche for life.

Another changing social area for young people is their relationships with adults. Junior highers want to be treated as older, to have more freedom and to make their own decisions. This push for independence may lead to heated arguments with Mom and Dad. At the same time, however, most still tend to be very family oriented. In their major study, Merton and Irene Strommen found that early adolescents had a strong desire for a close family.[16] Recent studies by the Barna Research Group show that "family is a big deal to teenagers, regardless of how they act or what they say. It is the rare teenager who believes he or she can lead a fulfilling life without complete acceptance and support from their family."[17] And junior highers will listen to adults and even obey teachers, coaches, youth leaders and other authorities if spoken to firmly and not in anger.

Early adolescents are very vulnerable socially. All their feelings and frustrations from the changes in their lives seem to be focused in this area.

Psychological Growth

According to Erik Erikson's classic stages of psychological development, the focus of the school age (approximately ages 6 to 12) is industry versus inferiority. "Industry" means a sense of competence. In other words, the child needs to feel that he or she is good at something.

In the next stage, adolescence (approximately ages 13 to 18), the focus is identity versus confusion. Here the young person is working on self-concept and answering the questions, Who am I? And where do I fit in?

Top Twenty Worries of American Young Adolescents

1.	School performance	57%
2.	About my looks	53%
3.	How well other kids like me	48%
4.	Parent might die	47%
5.	How my friends treat me	45%
6.	Hunger and poverty in U.S.	38%
7.	Violence in U.S.	36%
8.	Might lose best friend	36%
9.	Drugs and drinking	35%
10.	Might not get good job	30%
11.	Physical development	26%
12.	Nuclear destruction of U.S.	25%
13.	Parents might divorce	22%

14.	That I may die soon	21%
15.	Sexual abuse	19%
16.	Friends will get me in trouble	18%
17.	Drinking by a parent	15%
18.	Getting beat up at school	12%
19.	Physical abuse by parent	12%
20.	That I might kill myself	12%

—Merton P. and A. Irene Strommen, *Five Cries of Parents*[18]

Although the timing of these two stages varies widely, it is clear that *early* adolescence falls right in the middle of them. Thus, most junior highers, especially the younger ones, will be experimenting—trying athletics, music, art and other school activities—and working on their life skills. They want a sense of accomplishment. And some of the older ones will be trying on different identities, attempting to discover and understand who they are. *Am I an athlete? Am I a leader? Am I good looking? Am I smart? Am I shy?* These struggles consume much of a young person's emotional energy.

Incidentally, because young adolescents haven't fully developed their identities, most programs designed for high school students will not be effective with them. Instead, junior highers need activities and classes that will help them accomplish and achieve, to feel competent. Using high school programs with junior high (or combining both groups) is a mistake.

The New Nightmares

Teens themselves are well aware that they face threats that earlier generations didn't confront. Asked to rate the top threats to youth today, teens cite drugs, AIDS, school violence, and peer pressure. But the picture shifts when teens are asked about their personal concerns. Then, teens cite the same worries that adolescents have fretted about for decades—their grades, their looks, and getting into college. —David Whitman, "The Youth Crisis"[19]

The avalanche of changes also affects their emotions, and the ups and downs can be extreme. One of the causes for the emotional roller coaster is physical, as hormones kick in. In addition, there are mental, psychological, social and physical factors. Kids fear rejection; and they often feel misunderstood, left out, ugly and stupid. How would you feel if the girl you liked was a foot taller than you, your friends called you "runt," and the teacher laughed when he asked you to stand up? Or consider your elation when you discover through your best friend, Jolene, that Brett (the totally good-looking new guy) likes you.

Early adolescents, especially girls, let you know how they feel. And their emotions indicate what is going on inside.

Spiritual Growth

Let's face it. Talking about God in junior high just isn't cool. For kids trying to grow up, religion is often seen as something for little children or religious types. Many churches have confirmation or catechism classes for children. The purpose of these classes is to teach church doctrine and to confirm them in the faith. Ironically, however, confirmation often leads to a quick exit from church. It's as though the parental pressure comes off and the young person says, "All right. I went to the classes for you. Now that it's over, I'll do what *I* want to do."

One of the problems is that these classes tend to be very conceptual and irrelevant to real life and, thus, extremely boring. Students may memorize Bible verses and creeds, but often they don't understand what the verses and creeds mean or how they fit into their lives. Junior highers need to see how faith makes a difference in the real world. They need to see models of faith, and they need a place where they can voice their doubts and disbelief.

For those outside the influence of any local church (the vast majority of early adolescents), the spiritual realm can seem quite fuzzy. They may wonder about God or become curious about the occult. Whatever their background or interest, however, they are biblically illiterate. This is even true for many church kids too.

The gap is growing between the evangelical world and the rest of society, which is becoming increasingly secular. This secularization is obvious in the younger generation. In sixth grade my daughter invited one of her friends to attend church with us. Amy came from a nice suburban family. I had spoken with her father and knew that his background was Lutheran. But after the service, Amy said that it was the first time she had ever gone to church. And this happened in one of the most churched communities in America.

Most early adolescents live in a spiritual vacuum. They are hungry for something but don't know why or what to do about their hunger.

Greatest Problem

The following graph shows responses given when a group of young people were asked what they feel is the biggest problem facing people their age. Columns add up to more than 100 percent because some teens named more than one problem. [20]

	1992	1991	1987	1985	1983	1977
Drug abuse	40%	49%	54%	40%	35%	27%
Alcohol abuse	7	11	12	14	10	7
AIDS	11	6	5	0	0	0
Teenage pregnancy	9	10	11	3	0	0
Sex	6	4	*	*	*	*
Crime, teen gangs	6	9	*	*	*	*
School problems	5	3	1	4	5	3
Getting along with parents	2	2	2	2	5	20
Problems in growing up	2	1	2	5	1	6
Financing college	2	3	1	3	1	0
Unemployment	1	2	2	8	16	6
Fear of war	0	*	1	2	4	0
Economic problems	1	2	1	3	2	3
Career uncertainties	1	1	0	0	3	3
Teenage suicide	*	1	2	3	0	0
Miscellaneous	4	8	5	7	5	12
Don't know	6	12	8	13	18	14

* Less than half of 1 percent

Why Minister To Junior Highers?

- They are thinking through adult issues although they are still children; they need adults who will accept them, affirm them and let them enjoy life.
- They are experiencing tremendous physical changes which can be very confusing; they need support and encouragement.
- They are at an age of personality and character formation; what better time to reach young people for Christ?
- They are under increasing academic and moral pressure; they are vulnerable and need support.
- They are forming values and asking questions about life; they need answers from God's Word.
- They are very impressionable and still accept adults as models for lifestyle and values; they need us to offer friendship, love and positive role models.
- They are going to the same heaven or hell as adults; they need Christ.

Junior highers desperately need help navigating through these difficult years. They need concerned and caring adults who will spend time listening, loving, watching and teaching them—and who will lead them to Christ.

Are you that kind of person? Will you take the challenge?

Think *It* Through

1. What evidence have you seen recently to support the statement that children are hurried?

2. What are the most popular teenage radio stations in your area? List three of the top 10 songs on the pop charts right now.

3. Which junior highs do the early adolescents in your church attend?

4. What temptations might a junior higher face in a typical school day?

5. Imagine that a young person shares with you a problem that he or she is facing. Describe what that problem might be.

6. What might you say to help or encourage him or her?

7. What young people might possibly come to you for help? Why?

Chapter Three

Now What Do We Do?

Parable

Since as far back as he could remember, John wanted to be a builder. During childhood, his daydreamed occupations included carpenter, architect, general contractor, civil engineer, bricklayer—his imagination catapulting him into each newly discovered construction opportunity. And although John's adult career track had taken a different direction, he still harbored that secret ambition.

Then one day he saw that he had the chance to realize those childhood dreams. There was time (two weeks of vacation); there was space (his backyard); there was money (his special projects funds were ample). So, after a trip to the lumberyard to select only the finest wood, nails and other supplies, John gathered his tools and began to build.

Measuring, sawing and nailing, John worked as one obsessed, stopping only for food and sleep. Slowly his dream rose and spread across the yard. *I'm a builder!* he thought as he fell into bed each night, exhausted but exhilarated by the idea.

Of course, John's project was the talk of the neighborhood. The sights, sounds and obvious expense were impressive. Then after two weeks, the hammering subsided, and John's neighbors gathered at his fence to look and comment on his project.

"He sure worked hard," said one.

"What dedication!" said another.

"And I don't think I've every seen such wonderful workmanship," added a third.

"Just look at those beautiful boards!" said someone else.

But what is it? they thought. And no one knew—not even John.

The moral of the story: Before you begin, be sure you know what you're building.

Preamble

Assuming that you are convinced of the need to minister to early adolescents and of your ability to play a significant role in that ministry, the next step is to think through what you hope to accomplish. It may seem obvious, but too many youth workers, following their dreams, rush off to buy shiny new supplies and tools and begin working without knowing what they want to build. Their motives are pure, their commitment and dedication are commendable, and their materials are of the highest quality. But the results are amorphous structures, lacking definition and direction.

That's what this chapter is about—helping you develop a purpose, philosophy and plan for your ministry.

Process

Whatever the project or program, it is important that you follow this three-step process: purpose, philosophy and plan.

Purpose

Simply stated, the purpose is the ultimate goal of your work—what the final product will look like. John wanted to build something, but he wasn't sure *what* he wanted to build. A house, a skyscraper and a bridge differ greatly in their construction. The kind of structure chosen determines the expense, materials, tools, time and methods that will be required.

The most startling result of my research was the discovery that teens today are a "tribe apart" not because they have declared themselves as separate and different from adults, which, of course, has been a <u>perennial</u> part of the adolescent lifestage. Teens today are a tribe apart because the adult world has abandoned them. —Patricia Hersch, "A Tribe Apart: America's Teenagers"[1]

The same could be said about youth work. Although it is possible to have more than one goal (or structure) for a group or specific young person, it is important to spell out each goal individually. Be sure to discuss your goals with church leaders and parents to make sure that you are all heading in the same direction. Possible goals could include the following: to lead young people to Christ, to help young people grow in their faith, to help early adolescents resist the pressures and temptations of the junior high years, to build within junior highers feelings of competence and self-esteem, to teach young people basic life skills, and so forth.

After choosing a goal (or goals), write a simple purpose statement. If, for example, your goal is evangelism, you could write "The purpose of this ministry is to help junior highers trust Jesus Christ as Savior."

Of course, in order to decide your goals, you should have a good understanding of the young people with whom you will be working. I work with early adolescents at a church where I head the junior high ministry team. Because of the setting, the fact that all of the kids profess to be Christians and the need they have for knowing how their faith applies during this difficult time in their lives, our purpose statement reads "To help students understand how faith in Jesus Christ should change their lives." Sunday School is the main program already in place to help reach that goal.

In addition to discerning the vision, you must have a well-conceived plan for implementing it. A vision without plans is just a dream without a prayer. Plans make the vision practical and realistic. It has been said that those who fail to plan, plan to fail. Experience bears this out. While a good plan must be flexible, to achieve great things for God, you should create a schedule of time, resources, and activity that lead to the outcomes described by your vision. —George Barna, *Third Millennium Teens*[2]

We also realize that outreach is important, giving these kids the opportunity to bring their friends to a place where they can hear the gospel. So another goal of the ministry is "To motivate and provide opportunities for Christian students to reach their friends for Christ." To help reach this goal, we have a youth group that meets every other week in members' homes, Mystery Trips (trips to unannounced locations such as bowling alleys, miniature golf courses, etc.) and special events.

Another purpose statement for our group is "To teach and encourage young people to serve others." To help meet this goal, we sponsor an annual service project.

I also used to work with early adolescents in the neighborhood through Campus Life/JV (Youth for Christ's ministry for junior highers). Because this ministry is a direct response to the vast world of non-Christian young people, its purpose is preevangelism and evangelism. The program, then, is designed to address that purpose.

Philosophy

In this step you identify your ministry nonnegotiables. This means determining what you believe about ministry, young people and how they should be treated. Your philosophy should be consistent with your purpose. The philosophy of your ministry affects the way you perform ministry. Your program design should reflect this philosophy, and the curriculum and other materials you use should be consistent with it.

My philosophy of ministry includes the concept that youth ministry must be *relational*. In other words, leaders should build relationships with young people, spending time in the junior highers' world, getting to know them, becoming their friend. I also believe that any classes or studies should be *scripturally sound* and *practical*, helping them apply the Bible to their lives. Another important tenant is that the ministry must *support the family and the church*. You can see how these tenets of my philosophy of ministry would affect my ministry plan.

Plan

The plan is the actual design of the program—what you will do, consistent with your philosophy, that helps you achieve your purposes, or goals. Your plan could include how staff members (volunteer and salaried) spend their time; what activities, events, meetings, groups, etc. you will sponsor; and what facilities and materials you will use.

First think through your overall strategy; then plan specific events. Every activity should have an objective. For each event you plan, create a purpose statement explaining how that event ties into your overall ministry goals. Each ongoing program, as well as individual event, should have an objective.

As I mentioned earlier, the Sunday School program in our church is designed to reach our goal of helping young people understand how faith in Christ can change their lives. This purpose is stated in our objective for junior high Sunday School. The objective for each individual class, then, should tie into the overall objective of the Sunday School program. Objectives should be concise, specific and measurable.

Let's say that I am teaching a Sunday School class, and we are studying the Gospel of Luke. This Sunday we will discuss the story in chapter 17 where Jesus heals the 10 lepers, but only one returns to thank him. My objective could be "As a result of this lesson, my students will write a thank-you list to use in their prayer time." That objective is specific, action-oriented and consistent with our purpose for Sunday School.

One of the program objectives of Campus Life/JV is to teach young people life skills, and one of these skills is how to make friends. The topic for the first meeting in this series is how to meet friends. The objective is "As a result of this meeting, young people will list three to five places to find potential friends." Again, this objective is specific and involves action.

Objectives do not have to be action oriented. Knowledge objectives, in which the focus is on teaching content, can also be effective. One such knowledge objective might be "As a result of this meeting, students will know that Jesus rose from the dead." The Resurrection is an important biblical and historical truth that young people should know; therefore, this would be a good objective.

Keep in mind that lesson objectives should be measurable. You should be able to tell whether or not your meetings are successful, based on your objectives. A clear objective is important, not only because it keeps the activity in line with the overall purpose of the program, but also because it makes the rest of the planning process so much easier. The objective drives the event. It's like taking a trip in your car. If you know your destination is Indianapolis, you will travel on the roads that get you there.

You might think that all this talk about purposes, goals and objectives sounds complicated and involves a lot of busy work. It isn't and it doesn't. While it's true that at first this process may take some time, eventually it will become natural. In fact, before long, you will find yourself automatically asking yourself, *Why are we doing this activity? How does this meeting help us reach our goals?* Whatever your role in the ministry, I urge you to take time to think through and write out your objectives.

After writing your objectives, you will be ready to plan the rest of the activity. A simple outline for a plan might look like this:

WHAT? (the specific activity)
WHERE?
WHEN?
WHO? (the leaders and other ministry personnel)
HOW MUCH? (the costs and who will pay the bills)

Remember that the plan comes *after* the purpose and philosophy. Too many youth workers jump right into an activity or do something they enjoy doing, and then try to redirect the activity toward some unclear goal. The planning process requires much thought. A program shouldn't be chosen because we've always done it; because others are doing it; because it looks good on paper; or for any reason other than the fact that it is in line with your philosophy and will accomplish your purpose.

Principles

As you work through the purpose, philosophy and plan of your ministry, keep in mind the fact that there are several objectives that you should have for yourself.

Be Realistic

Beware of idealistic and unrealistic ministry goals and objectives. Remember that early adolescents have limited maturity, knowledge and experience. Don't expect them to learn more or do more than they can handle.

Somehow, I think, in my lifetime our evangelical community has made the disastrous mistake of encouraging children to go beyond their depth in theological understanding; the result may be that doctrines introduced too soon and at too young an age are relegated to the closet of discarded toys later in life. Part of the reason for this may be that we've gotten away from the catechism and similar gradual, structured learning methods. Another part may be our fear lest a child shall not have made a decision by age five or six.

I'm not saying that no child can find reconciliation to God through faith at that young age; many can and do. But even for them, the nails of the Cross, the crown of thorns, the deep things of our Christian faith may perhaps better wait for the development of conceptual thinking and experience in adolescence. If Jesus would receive the hardened criminal with the simple plea, "Lord, remember me when you come into your kingdom," surely he will receive a little child with a simple understanding of Jesus' love.

We're in such a hurry in contemporary America. And we're so inclined to interrupt to destroy childhood. —Joe Bayly, "God's in the Toy Box"[3]

The objective for a Sunday School lesson I read recently was to train students to share "The Roman Road" (a presentation of the gospel using verses in Romans) with their friends. Besides the fact that this particular witnessing tool is geared toward adults, the goal is still unrealistic for early adolescents. Most junior highers don't realize (or even *want* to know) that their friends are lost and need Christ.

This is especially true of younger students. In grade school, most of their classmates were good kids. A few may have caused trouble but nothing very serious. Most Christian children, then, assume that everyone is Christian (unless they are clearly Jewish, Hindu, Moslem or Buddhist). And most Christian children have no real understanding of denominations. When my daughter was in fifth grade, she commented one day that Melissa must be Catholic because her parents were strict and wouldn't let her listen to rock music. Later I found out that Melissa went to a Bible church and that her mom and dad were strong believers. Incidentally, my wife and I were more strict than they were.

Because junior highers haven't made clear Christian/non-Christian distinctions, a better objective would be that students learn that their friends need Christ. Then another lesson could discuss the best way to reach them. Eventually the class could cover how to carefully and lovingly explain the plan of salvation. All of this could be included under the life skill "how to explain what you believe."

Unrealistic goals for junior highers include expecting them to learn and understand the finer points of theology, to make a dramatic change in their families, to win their school for Christ, and to behave like adults. They may give the answers you want to hear or perform for you for a while, but inevitably early adolescents will act their age.

As youth leaders, it's also easy to get too optimistic about the results of our programs. For example, don't expect to have 100 kids show up to a pizza party when your usual attendance is 10. And don't expect everyone to listen attentively to everything you say. Your young people will move around, talk and make gross sounds—in other words, they will act like junior highers.

One night I was complaining to my wife about how the kids in JV wouldn't invite other people to the meetings. She commented that inviting others, especially a whole bunch of others, was a new concept to this age group. In all their activities so far, such as Brownies, gymnastics or soccer, kids signed up or joined. Gail suggested that instead of challenging kids to invite scores of acquaintances, I should encourage each of them to bring one or two of their close friends.

Of course, it's also possible to sell these young people short and to expect too little of them. For example, this age group can be very service oriented. That's why they enjoy working in the church nursery and babysitting. This interest and potential for serving others can be channeled into some very meaningful projects in the church and community. Recognizing this, many churches now have special mission trips for younger students.

Remember when designing your ministry to be realistic, keeping in mind the age and developmental level of the kids with whom you are working.

Be Relational

Jesus spent His entire public ministry training His 12 disciples. They walked, talked, ate and ministered together. In effect, He poured His life into them. And throughout the Gospels we see Jesus entering into conversations with and healing, loving, reaching out and touching individuals. The core of Christ's ministry on Earth was personal, building relationships with people and sharing Himself with them. Following Christ's example, we should be relational in our ministry.

We should also be relational because it is most effective. Books, magazines, television, radio, videos, booklets and large rallies can play a very important role in spreading the good news. All are helpful tools. But the most effective ministry happens person to person. Think of how you came to Christ. Who introduced you to Him and who has been most helpful in your growth in the faith? I remember godly parents, a sensitive pastor, Christian friends, a Sunday School teacher or two and a caring youth minister. *People* make the difference, and no paper or program can take their place. Remember, however, that these relationships should be moving in the direction of sharing Christ and biblical content (we'll discuss this in chapters 7, 9 and 10). George Barna asserts, "Providing relationships without spiritual substance results in turnover."[4]

Spiritual Dropouts

What is it about many current evangelistic methods that is so counterproductive to the goal?

1. A manipulative process tends to produce dropouts. This includes informative transmission (evangelism as a one-way communication of certain facts the hearer needs to know) and manipulative monologue (a sales pitch).
2. An evangelistic process that sees its goal as decisions rather than disciples tends to create dropouts.

3. An evangelistic process that presents the gospel one time and then asks for a response tends to create dropouts.

4. An evangelistic process that does not build relationships with the local church, its programs, and its ministry tends to produce dropouts.

—Win and Charles Arn, "Closing the Evangelistic Back Door"[5]

Junior highers are social animals. As mentioned in chapter 2, much of their time revolves around gaining and maintaining friendships. They need people who accept them as they are and care about them. And because they are changing in how they relate to their parents, they need adults who take time to listen to them and to tell them the truth. Be one of those adults for them. Make your ministry personal—be relational. (In chapter 6 we will examine more closely how to relate to junior highers at a personal level.)

Be Responsible

Irresponsible people don't care about what they do as long as they get results. And there are many irresponsible men and women in business, politics and even the Church, who have left a trail of destruction as they have pushed, pulled, clawed and climbed to the top.

Being a responsible minister to junior high young people means that you handle them with care, refusing to manipulate them for your own purposes, even if those purposes sound noble.

The visiting evangelist stood before the assembled Sunday School classes. Fifty pairs of eager and innocent childhood eyes gazed at him as he began to speak. Graphically he portrayed the wonders of heaven and the horrors of hell. Next he asked everyone to bow their heads and close their eyes. He paused for a moment and then broke the serious silence with a question. "How many of you want to stay out of hell?" He spat out "hell" with a snarl. "Raise your hands." Fifty hands shot up. "You can put them down," he continued. "And how many of you want to go to heaven?" The same fifty hands shot heavenward—it was unanimous. The evangelist concluded by leading the group in a prayer, assuring them that they had been saved. Then he left and recorded "50 decisions for Christ" on his personal statistics ledger.

That's manipulation, and it's irresponsible. The truth is that we could get most young children and even early adolescents to do almost anything we wanted them to do if we pushed the right emotional buttons. But that wouldn't be responsible, and it wouldn't be Christian. An overemphasis on competition can also be irresponsible. It's all right to reward kids, but don't get carried away. Being responsible means understanding where these young people are emotionally and handling them with care.

Because most junior highers are biblically illiterate (especially outside of the Church), much of our work will be preevangelism, laying the foundation and building a framework for the gospel. We want young people to make real, solid and life-changing decisions for Christ. We don't want them to respond out of peer pressure, emotional manipulation or a desire to please us. Remember whose needs you are trying to meet and be responsible in your ministry methods.

Be Real

I have three brothers, and we differ greatly. But we have one thing in common—we're all like Dad. Why? Besides genetics, this is due to the fact that he was our model of what it meant to be a man and a father. I found myself repeating *his* encouragements and warnings to my children.

 Our children will follow our example, whether good or bad. They will adopt our values. The major moral decisions they make will be shaped by the values they learn from Mom and Dad. If we love cars, houses, clothes, money, or sports, so will they. If we love winning more than playing well, so will they. And if we follow God unreservedly, chances are they will too.
—Bill Perkins and Dr. Rod Cooper, *Kids in Sports*[6]

We all model values, what is important to us. In fact, we cannot *not* model values. Values are communicated by how we act and react. Consider how you would react to a damaged book as compared to a dented car. You probably would get much more upset about the dented car. The car is worth more to you. That's a value. We also shout our values by how we spend our time, how we spend our money and how we treat people.

Early adolescents need to see *real* Christians working out their *real* faith in *real* life. As mentioned earlier, these young people still look up to adults. We can have a powerful influence in their lives. They are watching us to see what values we demonstrate.

I still remember an experience I had at summer camp when I was a kid. We were playing Balloon Stomp in a field. That's the game where everyone ties a balloon to his or her ankle and then tries to pop everyone else's balloon while protecting his or her own. Early in the game, our youth director's balloon was popped. Instead of dropping out, as the rules required, he continued to run around the field popping balloons. He was cheating. Whether he was just being immature or didn't want to lose, he made an impression. I'm sure he forgot that incident decades ago, but I never did, and I've found it difficult to respect him since then. He told us how *we* should live, but he didn't do it.

Being real means living what we preach, and it means being vulnerable. It is important, therefore, for you to be open and honest with students about your struggles and successes in the Christian life. Let them see your love for your spouse and children; let them see your love for the Church; and, above all, let them see your love for Christ.

Be Relevant

When discussing the development of junior highers earlier, I mentioned that the focus of this age group is on competence, achieving, being good at something. Your ministry should reflect this need. If you talk about intimacy (the emphasis of young adults) or about identity (the emphasis of late adolescents), your message will go right over their heads. Instead, you should minister where they are and teach them needed life skills.

The peer group is influential today largely by default. Young people today as in the past need a "bridge" to maturity, a smooth transition from childhood to adulthood. And in most cases the only bridge available is the peer group.

But teenagers today still desire acceptance and guidance from the adult community. They still need and want adult models who they can imitate and emulate. They want someone they can look up to. —Wayne Rice, "Every Kid Needs an Adult Friend"[7]

For many years I worked with high school students in Campus Life. Many of our discussions centered on topics like cliques, self-concept, sex and dating, the future, family, loneliness and so forth. The subjects were conceptual, felt-need oriented and focused on identity. In junior high, however, the focus had to change, because the kids were different. So we concentrated on teaching them life skills. (We will discuss the concept of life skills further in chapter 9.) Make relevance a priority as you minister to junior highers.

There is a danger when the process and product are confused. Values cannot be demonstrated; they are modeled in everything said and done. Skills are not modeled; they are demonstrated and taught. One word of caution: You cannot choose which values to model—modeling conveys all the values you hold, both good and bad.

Values are being eroded in our society. Recently Christians have emphasized the importance of modeling because we know that values must be conveyed to our young people in order for them to survive the world's temptations. Consider these questions:

- What values do you want modeled for your children?
- What values do you not want modeled for your children?
- What skills do you want your children to have?

—Dr. Bruce B. Barton and Dr. James C. Galvin, "Can We Take Modeling Too Far?"[8]

Be Resourceful

Hundreds of resources are available to you as a youth worker—use them. We are living in the age of technology and information—take advantage of that fact. More youth ministry tools are available now than ever before, so there's no excuse for having dull classes and boring meetings. (In the back of this book I've listed many of the books and other ministry tools currently available to youth workers.) And if you don't like the resources you've seen, write your own.

What I am suggesting is that you not *assume* anything when it comes to specific programs, activities and events. Try something new. Do something off the wall. Be creative. Who says your Sunday School class always has to meet in the same room with the chairs arranged in the same way? Who says your youth group always has to meet at the same time and place? Do whatever it takes, consistent with your philosophy of ministry, to achieve your purposes.

And try to catch kids by surprise. Some of our most popular events are Mystery Trips. We tell the kids to show up at church at a specific time, with a certain amount of money, and then we do something together. These aren't spectacular events, but they're special—and the kids love them. In the last couple of years, we have gone to a movie, had a scavenger hunt in a mall, played tennis (with lessons) at a sports center, had a treasure hunt and played laser tag and snow softball. The sky's the limit for your ministry! Use your imagination and be resourceful.

Be Ready

Teachable moments are often unpredictable. We never know when we will have the opportunity to model a value, reinforce an important lesson, or point someone to Christ. And we can't schedule crises—those tragic and stressful times. Therefore, we must be ready, as Peter says, "to give an answer to everyone who asks you to give the reason for the hope that you have" (1 Peter 3:15).

Of course, this means being available—we can't respond if we're not there. And it means being sensitive, listening carefully and watching for signals.

Charlene answered a question in Sunday School with a shrug of her shoulders and a disgusted sigh, "We're supposed to love our parents. That's the answer." It was obvious to me that there was something behind her words. Later I discovered she had a serious conflict at home.

During a trip to a water park, a couple of the guys came to me complaining about how one of them had lost a 10-dollar bill in the wave pool. Another boy had found the money but wouldn't give it back. After intervening, I discovered that the boy was friendly and quite willing to listen to reason. But I had to work hard to keep my kids from making this an angry confrontation and a test of egos. After we reached a solution, I was able to explain how their belligerent and argumentative attitudes had made the problem worse and how they could accomplish more by listening to the other person's side of the story.

Unfortunately, there are other times when teaching moments have slipped right past me. Later, looking back, I have seen how I could have taken advantage of teachable moments, but I wasn't prepared. Be ready.

Postlude

As vital as it is to minister to early adolescents, it is just as important to do it *right*. This means thinking through and developing your purpose, philosophy and plan.

Think *It* Through

1. List several possible purposes, or goals, of a youth ministry.

2. Which of these would be most appropriate for the youth with whom you will be working?

3. What are your ministry nonnegotiables? In other words, what principles would you include in your philosophy of ministry?

4. What young people have had the opportunity to spend concentrated amounts of time with you (at least an hour or two at a time)?

5. What are some of the values you communicated during this time?

6. What resources are available for you to use in your ministry?

Chapter Four

Parents:
Friends or Foes?

I don't know when the desire was implanted. I certainly had no lifelong, overwhelming feeling or obsession. Maybe it was because Mom and Dad were such great role models or because family times held such good memories. Whatever my subconscious motivation, I just knew that I wanted to be a father someday. I looked forward to cuddling beautiful babies ("He has your eyes!"), marveling at first toddling steps, teaching to throw and catch, watching and listening at recitals with justifiable pride, and recording every important event on film.

As newlyweds, Gail and I talked about starting a family, and we agreed to wait a few years to give ourselves time to establish our relationship. But we knew that when the time was right, God would give us children; and, of course, we would be terrific parents. But it wasn't easy having children. In fact, it seemed almost impossible to conceive, even though we tried everything we could. Nothing seemed to work.

Then one day Gail had a miscarriage. Although disappointing, this showed us that pregnancy was possible (we didn't even know she was pregnant at the time), and we saw it as a step in the right direction. Then after months of trying and hoping, Gail rushed home with the doctor's good news—she was pregnant again! A few weeks later, we felt confident enough to tell relatives and friends who rejoiced with us.

Only days after sharing the happy news, Gail walked into my office. I knew something was wrong—she should have been at school, and her eyes were red from crying. Then, rushing into my arms, she sobbed out those dreadful words: "The baby's dead. The baby's dead." Although I wanted to deny the test results from the hospital and the doctor's diagnosis, eventually I had to admit the truth. The fetus, our baby, had died; and we were back to square one in our efforts to become parents.

During the next few days and weeks, at times our grief seemed overwhelming. I remember crying out to God at night, "What's wrong? What have we done? Don't You trust us?" I knew of pregnant teenagers having conceived in the back seat of a car. And here we were, mature Christian adults, dedicated to God's service—and we couldn't have children.

Eventually Gail became pregnant again; however, the pregnancy was very difficult. During those nine months, she had to be very careful—no traveling, no lifting and no pushing and a lot of rest. In addition, Gail had a bad reaction to salt, a gall bladder attack, a case of shingles and, eventually, back labor. In the hospital, the doctor told me that Gail had what was then called acute toxemia. Later I learned that because of the poison in Gail's system, the baby had been losing weight, and both she and Gail could have died.

But on May 30, 1975, Kara burst into our lives. She was our five pounds of miracle, nestled in a pink blanket. Pain and problems forgotten, we marveled at our tiny, soft, innocent and wrinkled gift from God—the most beautiful baby in the world!

Gail and I dreamed of what Kara would become. We had such plans and hopes! As Kara lay in Gail's arms in the hospital, we would talk about her and pray for her. And she never seemed to cry when she was with us. I tried to sum up our wonder, our love, our thankfulness in a birth announcement poem for Kara Beth:

Welcome

Daughter or son
Soon to be one
God's gift to our home

The family tree
Will then be three
As you bid shalom

Baby's a word
Seldom's been heard
Save in whispered prayers

As miracle passed
You came at last
Transposing our cares

Tiny, soft, new
One made from two
As He did allow

And so it seems
All of our dreams
Rest with you now

Beginnings profound
Potentials abound
Alive from above

Parents we're now
But only know how
To give you our love

At home, however, it was different. Kara had colic and wore us down and out with 24 hours of wailing interruptions. But even at 3 A.M., struggling to stay awake and get her back to sleep, I would pray about Kara's future and wonder what lay ahead. *Would she be musical, athletic, intelligent, beautiful?* And there was the almost overwhelming feeling of inadequacy. *I'm a rank amateur at parenting! How can Gail and I ever raise this fragile newborn into a woman of God?* I wondered between lullabies and prayers.

During those sleepless nights, I also learned about unselfish love and gained a new appreciation for my parents. I thought of what they must have done and felt at my birth—and how much of their love I had taken for granted over the years. I looked into Kara's tiny, innocent eyes and whispered, "You will never know, Kara, how much we love you, how much you mean to us, until you go through this yourself and have children of your own."

My adventure in parenting began there and continued through the teen years. Many of my prechild, idealized dreams and ideas have materialized. But in the midst of moments of wonder, joy and excitement, there have been questions, doubts, fears, disappointments and struggles.

That's what it means to be a parent, not just for Gail and me, but for all the parents I know. So much of us (probably too much) is wrapped up in our children—love, dreams, hope and even identity. I would die for my girls, and I am very concerned about anything or anybody who would influence them.

That's why the key to junior high ministry is parents. You will have to work with them and through them if you want to work effectively with their children.

They Care

I know there are abusive parents who harm their children emotionally and physically, and there are others who don't care what happens to their children. But I think most parents *do* care and want only the best for their kids.

When I began working with high school students through Campus Life in the '60s, suspicious parents wondered if I was a Communist. In the '70s, especially in the wake of Jim Jones, the Moonies and others, the parents questioned whether or not Campus Life was a cult. And in the '80s and '90s, with stories of kidnappings and child pornography, parents wondered if I was a pervert or some dirty old man. Although the suspicions changed over the years, the motives were the same—parents wanted to know who was working with their kids.

There are four essential elements for a close family life. When present, they serve as a source of strength for adolescents. They are
1. Parental harmony
2. Parent-youth communication
3. Parental discipline or control
4. Parental nurturing
—Merton P. and A. Irene Strommen, *Five Cries of Parents*[1]

At first, I was threatened by the questions and insinuations. But then I learned to thank those parents who called to find out more about me. Their calls showed that they cared. They also helped me realize that working with other people's children is a heavy responsibility.

They Make a Difference

Although many parents begin to retreat from their kids at this age, those who hang in there have a profound influence in their children's lives. According to George Barna, in response to a question about influence in their lives, 78 percent of teenagers polled reported that their parents had "a lot of influence."[2] In fact, studies continually show that parents have more influence than peers do in the following areas: whether to attend college, whether to attend religious services, whether to do homework, and whether to drink. Parents also had an impact on the teens' job or career plans.[3]

If parents take a lively, though not defensive, interest in their children's lives, their teens are less likely to commit crimes, use drugs, or become pregnant prematurely. For example, teenagers who have dinner with their families most nights are far less likely to get into trouble than those who do not. Yet, the pressures on both parents and teenagers are in the other direction: toward immersion in work to support the overhead, not the essence, of family life.[4]

Handle Them With Care

Early adolescents are still relatively young—just out of grade school—so most parents still see them as their little boys and girls. Parents, therefore, will tend to be much more protective of children at this age than when they are in high school—when they are driving and doing much more on their own.

Parents are most sensitive about the oldest child. Having read and heard about all the problems that young people face, they are fearful about what will happen to *this* child and at the prospect of having a teenager in the house.

Communicate

Parents (especially good ones) want, and deserve, to know *who* is working with their son or daughter, *why* we are interested in him or her, *what* we will be doing, *how* they will be supervised and *when* the activities begin and end. First and foremost, safety tops the list of their concerns.

When I lived in Louisiana, every December during Christmas vacation, we would take a couple hundred high school students to Gatlinburg, Tennessee, for Youth for Christ's Winter Holiday. Our brochure was geared to kids, so it featured winter sports, great music, opportunities to meet new friends and fun. But we also sent a letter to the parents of those who registered or expressed interest. In this letter we gave the daily schedule, explained who the counselors were and how many young people each one would be responsible for, described the transportation, outlined the rules and the specific punishments for breaking them and even explained the emergency medical procedure. We wanted the parents to know that, although the trip would be fun, it would also be safe.

Anyone working with junior highers should communicate continually with parents. You can do this through letters, e-mail, newsletters, phone calls, parents' meetings and face-to-face encounters.

Relate

Of course the best way to head off a problem or diffuse any potentially explosive confrontation is to get to know a person and gain his or her confidence. This is especially important with parents. What you don't want is for them to ask and then answer their own questions. You should make yourself available to answer any questions that arise.

If you are young (for example, a student, just out of college, or in your late twenties), let parents know that you don't have all the answers, but you love kids and want to help them. Assure parents that you are always open to their suggestions and will keep your conversations with them confidential. If you are an older adult, especially if you have kids of your own, you will be able to talk with parents as peers, sharing common experiences and discussing parenting ideas. In either case, don't be afraid of parents. Treat them with respect and see them as allies.

Just trying to decide when to hold on and when to let go is enough to drive any normal parent into a state of terminal stress. So maybe the solution is not to worry about it. Perhaps the answer is that simple. We just keep the relationship constant. Despite all her running around to avoid us at the concert, despite all her pleas for her own TV set so she won't have to be in the same room with us, despite all her plans for an "unchaperoned" party at our house, we just keep going on about this business of being parents just as we always have. We won't panic. We won't yell. We won't even demand our rights or threaten her with independence since that is what she seems to want. We will just keep loving her and letting her know that we love her.
—Dr. Cliff Schimmels, *When Junior Highs Invade Your Home*[5]

Enlist Their Support

High schoolers are much more independent than younger students if for no other reason than the fact that they can drive. They don't have to depend on buses, parents or car pools to take them to school and to various activities. Although Mom and Dad are nervous when Junior gets his driver's license, they appreciate not having to be the chauffeur, carting him and his friends all over town. High schoolers are also breaking away from home in other areas as their parents give them more freedom. When I worked with high school students, I could take them out for Cokes after school, arrange to meet them at various locations and schedule activities at times that were best for them.

Consider the differences with junior high young people. First of all, they depend almost totally on their parents for transportation. Unless the place is close enough for them to walk or ride their bikes (during the day) to, someone, usually Mom or Dad, will have to drive them. This means that activities have to mesh with the family's schedule, not just the individual's. Parents are also concerned about their children having adequate rest and time for homework, so they protect their children's schedules. Remember, these are transition years for both parents and children.

My point is that parents are the gatekeepers. They have the responsibility and the power to control what their children do, all the way through junior high. And believe me, as a parent, it's easy to say no. Unless they know you and are sold on your program, they won't be of much help.

But this parental power can also be an advantage. If you gain parents' confidence and convince them that your program is just what their sons and daughters need, they will make sure their children attend. Whether it's Sunday School, youth group, Awana (nationwide children and youth Bible club), Campus Life/JV, WyldLife (the Young Life junior high program) or a special event, sell the parents on it and the kids will be there.

This means that you will have to design your publicity on two levels. With the kids, emphasize the adventure, excitement, fun and friends. With the parents, emphasize the content, values, relationships and leadership. Let mothers and fathers know that you are working with them to help their children grow mentally, socially, emotionally and spiritually. Show them that you're on their side.

Get Their Strengths on Your Team

Parents can be a tremendous asset to your ministry. If possible, recruit parents to serve on the ministry team. (I will discuss this further in chapter 5.) Remember, at this age young people are quite open to adults— even their parents. Some people think that kids don't like having their parents in meetings or at activities. That may be the case in certain situations, but I have found that generally the opposite is true. In fact, having Mom or Dad involved tends to enhance the relationship between parent and child. (If you're in doubt, ask the young person about it.)

It seems to me that if youth ministry is to continue to thrive, we need to be doing more and more with parents.

I had parents on my volunteer team. Best move I ever made! —Greg Lafferty, veteran junior high minister in Illinois and California and currently teaching pastor, Christ Community Church, St. Charles, Illinois

Automatic Access to the School

In the role of professional youth worker, I had to continually win the right to go on campus, even in schools where I had served for 13 years. Although I had developed a great relationship with the administration and faculty and had worked closely with them, I still was an outsider. One false move and I could be out on my ear. When I began to work with Campus Life/JV in my community, I couldn't believe the difference that being a parent made. When I walked through the doors of the middle school and into the office, I was Kara's father and received royal treatment. Everyone was polite and friendly, listening carefully and trying to assist me.

School administrators are very sensitive to parents, because the parents' children are in that building. When I spoke with the assistant principal about the JV program and told her that it was sponsored by a parent committee, she thanked me for what we were doing and offered the school facilities for our use. I was doing virtually the same thing that I had done in the high school ministry, but here they welcomed me.

A good relationship with school administrators is important for anyone who wants to have a personal ministry with young people. Sunday School teachers and others will have occasion to visit schools to pick up kids, talk with counselors, attend events and so forth. And remember, parents are always permitted to be at school.

Natural Contact with Students

As a young Campus Life staff member, I had to schedule my time carefully to be with students. This involved going on campus, watching practices and attending school events. We called this *contacting* and *building time*. Because relationship building requires time, I worked hard to be with the kids.

As a parent of a teenager, however, I was amazed at how much contacting would take place in the course of a week without even trying. One day, for example, I drove five girls to school; the next weekend, a couple of others were at the house; that Friday, Gail and I were chaperones for the school's activity night; I went to most of Kara's volleyball and basketball games; I would see tons of kids when I jogged though the neighborhood. Being with kids used to be part of my job—then it became part of my life.

Again, this contact is important for any kind of youth ministry. Even if you are only working with a small group of students at church, your involvement with them in the neighborhood and with their friends will help reinforce the values you represent, will encourage the young people to live for Christ and will help them reach out to friends.

Credibility with Other Parents

When parents learn that other parents are sponsoring and running a youth activity or program, they are much more willing to allow their children to become involved. I found this true both with Campus Life/JV and our church youth group. I wasn't someone they had to get to know. I lived in the white house on the corner, near the grade school; I was Kara and Dana's dad; we had seen each other at swim meets, PTA meetings, block parties, school activities and other community events. I wasn't a stranger—they knew me. And I was working at parenting just as they were.

Knowledge About Kids

All parents are amateurs—no one is an expert on how to raise his or her child. But all parents know a good deal about young people from personal experience.

Because I had a teenager living in my house, I was constantly involved in a real-life, youth ministry laboratory, learning firsthand what adolescents are like and how to relate to them. Of course, I was also learning how much I did *not* know, so I welcomed the advice and help of youth ministers and other parents.

Get Them Involved

Of course, not all parents should be on the ministry team. Some may not be Christians, be interested or have the ability. Even so, working with parents will provide other resources and opportunities.

Volunteer Time

Most parents of younger children are used to being asked to work as volunteer coaches, room mothers, swim-meet timers and other assorted roles for just about every activity in which their kids have become involved. And, as mentioned earlier, they drive their children everywhere. Most parents volunteer to help in some way, even if it's just to coordinate transportation.

When I signed up my daughters for soccer, a line on the form read "Where would you like to help?" and then it listed various options. Note that it did not ask "Would you like to help?"

This doesn't mean that parents have a lot of free hours to donate. But they expect to be asked to help out—and usually will. Some have more time than others. Single parents, for example, will be much more limited, but still they will do what they can. Parents often approach me both at church and in the neighborhood and ask how they can help with my ministry.

Services

In addition to giving their time, most parents will gladly take their turn hosting meetings, bringing refreshments, driving, designing fliers, making phone calls and so forth. They know that these tasks are necessary and that they should do their part.

Spiritual and Moral Support

Christian parents are well aware of the spiritual needs of their child and his or her friends. I remember telling our associate pastor that, as a parent of a teenager and an almost teen, I ached for other Christian adults to be involved in my daughters' lives. I wanted them to have positive role models and to hear our values affirmed from others whom they admire and trust.

Moms In Touch is a good example of this concern. In this program, Christian mothers of students in a specific school will covenant with each other to pray regularly for their sons and daughters.

> It is a fact that most parents have a feeling of love toward their children. It is assumed, however, that parents naturally convey this love to a child. This is the greatest error today. Most parents are not transmitting their own heartfelt love to their children, and the reason is that they do not know how. Consequently, many children today do not feel genuinely, unconditionally loved and accepted.
>
> This, I feel, is the case in most children's problems today. Unless parents have a basic love-bond relationship with their child, everything else (discipline, peer relationships, school performance) is on a faulty foundation, and problems will result.
> —Dr. Ross Campbell, *How to Really Love Your Child*[6]

If we challenge Christian parents to pray, they will, and they will enlist others to join the prayer team. In organizing a new Campus Life/JV ministry in our neighborhood, our first step was to have a meeting of Christian parents. At this meeting, we didn't recruit to fill any of the volunteer positions on the ministry team. Instead we explained the ministry and challenged the parents to pray for the junior highers they knew in their homes, neighborhoods and churches. We felt that if all we did was motivate and mobilize parents to prayer, these meetings would be successful. Imagine the impact on your church if parents and others would pray regularly for the young people in the congregation and for your ministry with them.

Parents will also encourage us. They appreciate the fact that someone cares about their children. During one year at three neighborhood parties, a father said essentially the same thing to me on each occasion: "That's a really good thing you're doing with the JV program. Thanks." He wasn't from an evangelical church and didn't know all the subtleties of the ministry, but he knew what it meant to his daughter—and he was thankful.

Financial Support

As mentioned earlier, junior high parents are critically aware of the need for responsible ministry to adolescents. They see the need in their own homes as their junior highers grow up before their eyes. Therefore, they understand the ministry and are willing to support it—especially if they are involved personally as a member of the ministry team or as a prayer partner, driver or refreshment provider.

One day, one of my neighbors handed me $25 and explained that she wanted to help with our expenses. On another occasion, two fathers donated $150 to buy *Campus Life* magazine subscriptions for the graduating eighth graders. On a larger scale, one of the easiest budget items to gain approval for in our church is junior high ministry. Parents will help financially, because they know the need for the ministry and see its results

Open to the Gospel

As children enter early adolescence, parents become very sensitive to their own inadequacies and very open to suggestions and support. This is true for *all* parents, not just those in the Christian community. A junior higher could be the bridge for establishing relationships with these concerned or even hurting parents and eventually introducing them to Christ. You could have a parents' meeting; sponsor a parenting seminar; tell them about Focus on the Family, the Gathering of Men, and other adult ministries; give them copies of *Understanding Your Teenager*, the *Life Application Bible* and other resources; or invite them to church. As they get to know you and your ministry through their children, they will begin to trust you and be receptive to your loving witness.

Although parents can seem like the enemy, questioning our motives and analyzing our moves, we must realize that parents and youth workers are really on the same side. Working with parents is the key to successful junior high ministry. Instead of fearing and avoiding parents, we should get to know them, communicate with them, get them involved in the program and minister to them.

A mother once wrote to me for advice, having reached the end of her rope over the entertainment issue with her teenage daughter. Perhaps her cry for help sounds all too familiar: "I have been knocking heads with my 13-year-old daughter over the music issue. She resents me telling her which rock albums I will allow her to buy and listen to. I'm not her favorite person these days anyway, and I am afraid this issue is becoming a giant wedge in our relationship. What can I do?" —Robert DeMoss, Jr., *Teen Tune-Up: A Parent's Primer on Popular Youth Culture* [7]

Working with junior high young people offers you a rare opportunity to impact whole families for Christ because of the concern and commitment of parents. Don't miss it!

Top 10 Reasons to Start WyldLife

10. Provides financial growth by including more donors/parents of middle school kids.

9. Fulfills Young Life's mission statement of "introducing adolescents to Jesus Christ and helping them grow in their faith."

8. Grows stronger high school ministries.

7. Expands Young Life's influence and impact in kids' lives—and produces more Campaigners, work crew, summer staff, student staff, interns, and volunteer leaders.

6. By bringing caring adults into their lives, it could possibly help kids avoid destructive behavior at an earlier age.

5. Capitalizes on a unique period of openness to the Gospel and openness to accepting Christ.

4. Provides a faith-enriching leadership opportunity—particularly for high school Campaigners and college freshmen.

3. Expands Young Life's influence in a community and engages a new set of adults as leaders and committee members.

2. Forces Young Life to think more creatively about non-traditional camping opportunities.

1. Middle school kids will come to know Jesus in a real and personal way.

—Nicki Reno, "Wow! WyldLife"[8]

Think It Through

1. Imagine that you are the parent of a young person about to enter junior high. What would be some of your concerns and worries?

2. What might you think if your son or daughter came home from school and told you about an adult who was hanging around and talking with kids?

3. As a youth minister (volunteer or professional), what would you say to describe your ministry to a non-Christian parent?

4. For what tasks or ministry team roles do you think you could recruit parents?

5. List Christian parents who would be good candidates for serving on the ministry team.

6. List parents of junior highers who might be open to ministry in their own lives.

7. What could you do to minister to those parents?

Chapter Five

Building
the Team

Everyone is in place and set. Looking over the defense, the quarterback barks out his verbal code. The wide receiver goes in motion from right to left, shadowed by a defender in the defensive backfield. Suddenly bodies explode across the neutral zone, each man thrusting hundreds of pounds of muscle forward, trying to move and control his opponent. The left tackle blocks to the right, double-teaming the defensive lineman with the left guard. Pulling left, down the offensive line, the right guard hits the defensive tackle, pushing him out. At that precise moment, the quarterback, having faked a pitchout, hands the ball to the tailback who follows the fullback through the hole. The linebacker moves to fill the hole but is hit by the charging fullback. Cutting to the right off that block, the ball carrier is finally tackled by a defensive back after a nine-yard gain.

Football is a team sport. Although the quarterback, tailback and wide receivers get most of the credit for the offense, the success of each play depends on 11 athletes carrying out their assignments. Knowing this, the wise coach carefully selects team players whose abilities and strengths complement each other and then molds them into an efficient and effective unit.

Teamwork is also important in youth ministry. Of course, it is possible to reach young people by yourself, building relationships and sharing Christ with individuals, but you will be much more effective if you build a ministry team. Remember, even the Lone Ranger had Tonto.

The Value

The genius of any team is that the whole equals more than the sum of the parts. If I am working alone, I can accomplish a certain amount. If you help me, we can accomplish more than just double my work, especially if your abilities complement mine. Our planning, thinking, talking and lifting should increase our productivity more than twofold. Certain tasks in life may be best accomplished by the individual, but youth ministry is not one of them. The task is too great, the stakes are too high, and the message is too vital. The team approach also offers several advantages simply not available to an individual.

Multiplies Gifts
Romans 12:5,6 says that "in Christ we who are many form one body, and each member belongs to all the others. We have different gifts, according to the grace given us." Each Christian has a unique blend of natural abilities, developed talents and spiritual gifts. God can use each person's strengths to build up the Body of Christ and to reach others for Him. I know of no one who has every spiritual gift—not even full-time Christian workers. One person may be a creative, idea person; another may be a great

administrator; and someone else may be an excellent teacher. With a team approach, one person's strength can compensate for another's weakness.

Eases Workload

Youth ministry involves much time and effort, and even the most dedicated and talented individual will become exhausted trying to carry the load alone.

Fresh out of college and into full-time youth work, I was assigned three high schools to reach for Christ. Each of these schools had over 3,000 students, so my mission field numbered nearly 10,000. Needless to say, I felt overwhelmed. Your assignment may not be so broad, but it is still large. Even with a handful of young people, there are classes and events to plan, calls to make, parents to meet, school activities to attend and, of course, kids to relate to, challenge and counsel.

God tells us that "two are better than one, because they have a good return for their work: If one falls down, his friend can help him up. But pity the man who falls and has no one to help him up! Also, if two lie down together, they will keep warm. But how can one keep warm alone? Though one may be overpowered, two can defend themselves. A cord of three strands is not quickly broken" (Ecclesiastes 4:9-12). Team members can share the load.

Offers Variety

Having more than one person involved adds variety to a ministry. It's helpful for young people to see Christ at work in many lives and to hear the message from more than one source. On a personal level, not everyone relates to the same kind of individual. And because of where junior highers are socially and the special needs of each sex, it is best if women work closely with the girls and men with the boys.

This approach also gives team members variety. One person may help teach Sunday School for a quarter; then she might work with the youth group for the next few months. Altering assignments keeps a ministry fresh and gives leaders the chance to see kids in different settings.

Supplies Replacements

In the course of a year, situations arise that prevent people from carrying out their assignments—emergencies, sicknesses, vacations and so forth. When these inevitable interruptions arise, other team members can fill in and carry on the ministry. That's one reason why I have one member of the ministry team in charge of Sunday School, and he has a group of nine helpers. Two adults, including myself, and six college students work with the youth group. When I had to be out of town, the college students led the meeting. Team members cover for each other.

We also live in a very transient area. Many of our church members are transferred every three years, so our turnover rate for church responsibilities is very high. Having a ministry team protects us from leadership gaps and ensures continuity.

Who Volunteers and Why

- About 45% of adults 18 years of age or older reported volunteering in 1987.
- Time given to volunteer work averaged 4.7 hours a week.
- People 65-74 volunteered the most (6 hours a week), followed by those 45-54 (5.8 hours).
- People with household incomes of $20,000 to $30,000 volunteered most often, followed by those earning $50,000 to $75,000.
- People volunteered in order to do something useful (56%), because they would enjoy the work (35%), because a family member or friend would benefit (27%), or for religious reasons (22%).

—*Newsweek*[1]

Provides Support

Never forget that youth ministry is a battle—not with kids or parents (although it may seem that way at times), but with Satan. (Check out Ephesians 6:12.) In an effort to capture these young lives, he will throw obstacles and opposition at us to cause us to become discouraged with our ministry and give up. According to Ron Hutchcraft, president of Ron Hutchcraft Ministries in Harrison, Arkansas, "It's a battle for a generation." That's why we need prayer and encouragement. In fact, our first priority should be to enlist a group of men and women who will pray for the junior highers, for us and for the ministry. Because members of the ministry team know they are in the battle together, they support one another.

Selection

Most churches have more jobs than workers and more assignments than volunteers, so those in charge of a ministry area often recruit any available person to fill a vacancy. Some people volunteer because they feel guilty ("Well, I suppose I should—I haven't taken my turn yet"), others because they're naive and some because they can't say no. As a result, positions are often filled by people who are uncalled, unmotivated and unqualified; and this applies to all jobs—from serving on boards to teaching Sunday School.

Don't let that happen with the junior high ministry team. Instead, after informing the church of the needs and responsibilities of the ministry and challenging people to respond, choose carefully those you would have serve.

Three basic criteria to use when recruiting and selecting the ministry team are spirituality, motivation and talents/gifts.

Spirituality

Although it's not necessary to have a team of spiritual giants, those who minister to young people should have a mature and growing faith in Christ. In other words, they should be solid Christians who live what they profess and teach. Early adolescents are impressionable, and they watch us closely. We want them to see solid Christian values in our lives.

I once had a staff member who had been kicked out of a restaurant for being rowdy and abusive to a waitress. I'm sure that at the time the kids with him thought it was funny, but think of what they were learning about how to treat others and how to be an adult. And I could write another book about the young lives that have been devastated by the marital problems or moral failings of their leaders.

You can't know everyone's heart, nor can you guarantee anyone's spiritual success, but do your best to choose those who have a solid relationship with Christ.

A simple four-step formula can be used when full-time staff train volunteers, and also when volunteers train other volunteers. The first step in this learning process is explanation, which is followed by demonstration. The third step is the student explaining the skill to the teacher, which is a good check for understanding. Finally, the teacher should supervise the student practicing the skill. This helps the trainer know whether or not the person is on the right track.

Motivation

My parents' generation used the word "burdened" to describe a personal sense of God's calling someone to a specific ministry. And I can think of no better word to use here. Look for those who are burdened for junior high young people. You can hear the burden in their conversation and in their prayers. They have deep concern for this age group and want to reach them for Christ. Of course, burdened volunteers may be hard to find in this age of materialism and consumerism.

In Youth for Christ, our strategy for building a ministry team was to begin by identifying Christian parents of junior highers in a particular school district. Then, at a meeting, we would tell them about the need for the ministry and the structure of Campus Life/JV. We would also challenge them to pray for the junior highers they knew and for their possible roles in the ministry. These parent meetings were *not* sales pitches designed to recruit team members. In the discussions that followed, however, those who were burdened for young people quickly surfaced. We challenged *those* parents to be on the team.

That's why parents make such ideal team members. They are eyewitnesses to the need, *and* they care. Adults of any age can work with junior highers. Early adolescents have not yet turned off the older generation. In fact, most junior highers still respect and listen to their elders.

Your team could also include college students and even high schoolers. Junior highers almost idolize them. Older kids can have a great impact. Be sure, however, to use the same selection criteria for these students as you use with adults. They should be committed Christians, motivated to minister to this age group. Remember, you want them to be positive role models. Don't use the junior high ministry to keep older kids involved or as a way to force them to grow up.

How to Be a Successful Volunteer

Be sure you make a difference. Ask the group for its mission statement; then ask how the volunteer work fulfills the mission, says Nan Hawthorne, managing director of Sound Volunteer Management in Seattle. If volunteers are truly to make a difference, the agency should regularly meet with them—and listen when they have something to say. —Marc Silver, "Is Volunteering a Waste of Time"[2]

Talents/Gifts

This criterion is the least important of the three because the quality of the person is much more significant than his or her abilities. We should consider, however, the strengths that each person brings to the team. Some are good administrators but have trouble relating to young people on a personal level. Others, filled with enthusiasm and creativity, are terrific at running games and activities. Some may be good at leading and managing. And there are those who are gifted teachers.

To some extent, the people on the team will determine the specific areas of responsibility. But it also works the other way. In other words, your purpose, philosophy and plan may help you decide the team's configuration.

Structure

As you build the ministry team, it will be helpful to outline what is expected from each team member.

Time

Super volunteers exist who will put in 10 to 15 hours a week in youth ministry. Their commitment and energy are commendable, but they are the exceptions—and usually young and single!

Most people don't have that kind of time to give to the ministry and will say no to your request.

Three hours of service per week is much more realistic. This may not seem like much, but it will work if you have enough people and limit the scope of each responsibility. For example, if leading the youth group involves planning, publicizing and running all the weekly meetings, it will take much more time than three hours a week. If you divide those responsibilities among two or three people, however, each job can be managed. Another possibility is having the youth group meet every other week. This would also decrease the amount of time needed from each leader.

I am an active volunteer in my church and community. I serve on my college's alumni board and parent council, sing in the church choir, help with worship, occasionally teach adult Sunday School and serve as a church elder in addition to my junior high ministry involvements. Obviously the total amount of time required for these responsibilities is more than 10 hours a week. If any one of them had demanded that kind of time commitment, I would have refused. But because they came in three-hour increments (or less), I knew I could manage them, so I said yes—one request at a time.

The quality and commitment of volunteers do not diminish with the decrease in the time required. You can get a great volunteer for three hours a week.

Roles

To determine ministry roles, think through everything that has to be done. Then see if you can divide the responsibilities to match the interests and abilities of your team members. For the junior high ministry at church, we have about 10 volunteers who work with the Sunday School and nine who work with the youth group. In addition, one woman serves as our secretary, lining up homes for meetings, putting announcements in the church bulletin and sending out schedules. One man coordinates our special events, and another couple plans the Mystery Trips. Another couple heads up our mentoring program. My role is to lead the team and help with the youth group.

The following are the recommended volunteer positions and their descriptions for Campus Life/JV as we originally designed the ministry. Note that each one describes the task and the kind of person needed.

- Team Leader—This person recruits and supervises the other team members, runs staff meetings and may substitute if someone is gone; needs management and supervision skills.
- Emcee/Program Coordinator—This person leads the weekly meetings with the teacher and runs the games; needs up-front skills.
- Teacher—This person leads the weekly meetings with the emcee and presents the life skills each week; needs teaching skills.
- Personal Ministry Coordinator—This person matches young people with staff for counseling and ensures that follow through is taking place; needs personal ministry skills.
- Transporatation Coordinator—This person enlists parents and others to drive kids to the weekly

meetings and other events and lines up buses, vans, etc. when needed; needs organizational skills.

- Sponsoring Schoolteacher—This person represents the ministry on campus, serving as a liaison with administration and faculty and communicating with students through school announcements, etc; needs to work at the school.

Some groups have added other positions—secretary, refreshment coordinator, fund-raiser and substitute teacher, among others. You can divide the responsibilities almost any way you wish. Use your imagination.

A church in my community has a large junior high Sunday School department, so they have broken the large group down into small groups, each with six to eight kids and an adult leader. Another church found that for big events they needed a technical staff, team leaders and assistants, crowd controllers and a clean-up crew in addition to the regular ministry staff.

Most junior high groups are small. Regardless of size, the ministry should be divided into manageable units with well-defined responsibilities for each position. The positions on your ministry team should be determined by the structure of the program and the people available.

A useful tool in communicating roles with your ministry team is the one-on-one review. This is a 30-minute meeting in which you discuss with a volunteer how his or her ministry with the students is going. The following five-step outline is very helpful for knowing how to conduct the review:

1. Ask how the person is doing.
2. Read his or her ministry reports and give feedback.
3. Discuss problems and goals.
4. Develop an action plan.
5. Share prayer requests and pray together.

Whatever your situation, don't try to do it alone. You can't teach and manage even a small group of students at the same time. One youth ministry veteran tries to have an adult leader for every six kids.

> One of the most frustrating volunteer problems youth workers encounter is that junior high ministry attracts adults, of any age, who are actually kids. Some adults haven't completed their adolescence and are attracted by the lifestyle and antics of young teenagers. These adults are looking for acceptance and to some degree are continuing to try out new identity patterns themselves.
>
> While many youth workers enjoy being a bit juvenile at times (otherwise we probably wouldn't be interested ourselves in junior high ministry), it's important to find adults who enjoy being adults. —Scott Noon, "Shopping for Jr. High Volunteers"[3]

Supervision

Whether you are a professional youth worker or a volunteer team leader, much of the success of the ministry team will depend on how well you supervise them. Just remember the following four words beginning with *T*, and you'll do all right.

- "*Team*"—Make sure that everyone knows it's a team effort. You're all in it together. This means having staff meetings in which you fellowship, plan, troubleshoot and pray.
- "*Time*"—There's no substitute for relationships, but relationships take time. Get to know your team, and

let them know that you are available to talk and pray. Communicate regularly through meetings, phone calls, letters, e-mail, newsletters and personal conversations. A good relationship will also win you the right to be heard when you have to confront someone about a problem.

- "Training"—Volunteers often feel unqualified and even intimidated by the ministry. Be constantly on the lookout for books, videos and other resources that you can pass along to the team. Share your expertise with them; and, if the budget allows, send them to special seminars on youth work. Check the list of resources at the end of this book.
- "Thanks"—No matter how dedicated and committed he or she is, no one wants to be taken for granted. Let team members know that you appreciate them. Express your gratitude with a year-end dinner; books or other gifts; recognition in the bulletin, church newsletter and worship service; or frequent sincere thank-you notes. People need to know that they are valued. You can never say "Thanks" too often. Volunteers need this kind of attention and they deserve it.

Although it is far from being a game, youth ministry is a team sport. The team has no stars, just men and women who care about kids and use their gifts and abilities to reach them for Christ. Build the team with care and prayer.

Think It Through

1. What volunteer responsibilities do you now have? Which ones do you enjoy the most? Why?

2. Who recruited you to take that position? What convinced you to do so?

3. List the possible roles that your junior high ministry team could have.

4. List the people you know who would meet the criteria (spirituality, motivation, talents/gifts) and could be possible ministry team members.

5. To what youth ministry training resources do you have access?

6. What could you do to motivate and mobilize people in your church or community to pray for junior highers and the ministry?

Chapter Six

Getting Close

Thus far we've discussed what early adolescents are like, the need for working with this age group, how to get organized, the role of parents and how to build a ministry team. Now we come to the heart of the matter, relating to junior highers themselves.

In chapter 2, I said that ministry should be relational. In other words, the most responsible and effective way to reach young people is through getting to know them and building relationships with them.

This principle is not limited to youth work or even to ministry. Every day I receive a number of sales calls—through the mail, on the phone or even at my door. Almost always I toss the letter or say I'm not interested, before even hearing the pitch. But if a friend of mine writes, calls or stops by and wants to tell me about his exciting new product or service, I will hear him out. The relationship makes the difference. My friend has won the right to be heard.

Consider your spiritual journey. How were you won to Christ? Who has influenced you the most? Probably a person who cared. Other means of communication have their place as valuable tools. Broadcast and print media, for example, can support and reinforce the spread of the gospel. But the message must be personalized, carried and communicated by a person, a friend, someone known and respected.

You can design the sharpest brochures, sponsor the wildest activities, host the most creative and exciting meetings and even serve the tastiest refreshments—and you may attract large crowds. But without love, your efforts will be hollow (that's my paraphrase of 1 Corinthians 13:1). If your purpose is changing lives, you must build relationships.

An Outdoor Education

One May afternoon, Kara burst into the kitchen after school and breathlessly announced, "There's Outdoor Education coming up, and they need parents to come—so do you want to help?" Then, placing her book bag on the table, she reached in and pulled out a note from the school with the details. Outdoor Education was an annual overnight experience for fifth graders at a camp in Wisconsin (about an hour-and-a-half away). The schedule would include nature walks, initiative tests, group-building exercises and games. And because the two elementary schools involved feed into the same junior high these students would attend next year, the event would provide a good opportunity for them to get to know kids from the other school. Parent volunteers were needed to serve as overnight chaperones.

As a youth ministry veteran, I was used to camps, camping, kids and counselors, so I volunteered. *So what if I lose a little sleep,* I thought. *This will be a good opportunity to get to know these kids.* I was confident in my ability to relate, have fun and keep control.

When I arrived at the camp, just after dinner, I was assigned a cabin. The cabin had two large rooms, one on each side, joined by a common bathroom and a counselors' room. Boys from Brookdale Elementary (my school) were on one side, and boys from Longwood Elementary were on the other. My fellow counselor was a Longwood father and junior high teacher in another district.

Around 8:30 at night, everyone was told to head for the cabins. Lights out was at 9:30. Gathering our group in one room, my fellow counselor and I introduced ourselves and read the rules. Then I pulled out a couple of games that I knew they would enjoy. These crowd breakers had worked great with high schoolers.

But no one was interested. Instead, they wanted to play cards and throw things at each other, so I retreated from plan A and decided to control the chaos.

Around 9:15, I got their attention and explained what I expected of them. I tried the good-guy, friendly, reasonable approach that had worked on some high school retreats. I said that although I would turn the lights off at 9:30, I didn't care when they actually went to sleep as long as they were quiet and didn't keep anyone else awake. I smiled and tried to appeal to their goodwill and good sense. They all seemed to understand, so after everyone was in bed, I turned out the lights and went to my room.

The place erupted! In fact, every time I left them, they went wild. Obviously the friendly approach wasn't working.

Then, during one of the brief interludes when I had gotten them relatively quiet, I went to the room on the other side of the cabin. My fellow counselor was seated in front, like a prison guard, watching his group carefully. Anyone who disobeyed had to do a prescribed number of push-ups.

About that time I heard more noise from the guys on my side of the cabin. I was desperate, so I thought I would try my partner's approach. I pulled up a chair, acted as stern and tough as I could and meted out punishments to fit the crimes—the prescribed push-ups and so forth. What I couldn't believe was that the guys actually did what I told them. Think about it. I had no real authority to back up my words—I wasn't a teacher, principal or coach. I couldn't reduce a grade, give detention, reduce playing time or send them home. I was just a volunteer trying to keep the peace. And yet they obeyed.

Eventually, things quieted down and everyone went to sleep. As I lay in my bunk, I thought about how those boys probably saw me as a mean person, a bad guy. I felt sorry for Kara, because I knew they would tell her how terrible her father was.

But the next morning, they were friendly. We laughed together in the breakfast line and the worst offender the night before told Kara, "Your dad is really cool!" I couldn't believe my ears. I had done nothing *cool*. I hadn't even tried being funny and had given up being nice. I had just been a policeman, but this young man thought that was cool.

That experience was an outdoor education for *me*, and I began to learn how to relate to this age group.

Principles for Relating

Encourage every member of your ministry team to begin to relate on a personal level with the young people in your group. Some team members may only get to know one or two young people, but that will help. Here are some basic principles for relating to junior highers.

Be Adult

In my work with high school students, it took time to break down personal barriers and to build confidence with kids. Eventually they were comfortable enough to begin calling me "Dave." They knew I was an adult, but they felt free to be personal, so they called me by my first name. I related to them, especially the older ones, almost as peers. We talked about issues in the world and in their lives, thought through great concepts and ideas, and discussed the claims of Christ. But I probably couldn't have done that with junior highers. Early adolescents are different and need to be treated differently.

Junior highers still have a high degree of respect for adults and their authority. The boys in my cabin were ready to accept me, because I was Kara's dad and because I represented the school. And after spending just a short time with them, they even liked me. There weren't the same barriers that I had found in high school ministry.

I must also add that I've never enjoyed the same closeness with junior highers that I have with high schoolers, even those who have been in the program for two or three years. Although we've spent many hours together, they still relate to me as an adult. They call me "Mr. Veerman," but that distance or formality doesn't hinder communication. They'll never be my buddies, but we can be friends.

Building friendships with junior highers does not involve stripping yourself of your adulthood and somehow taking on the disguise of a kid, dressing a certain way and using current slang expressions. It does mean taking time to understand these young people—their ways of thinking, their language and their struggles. Junior highers haven't yet turned off the older generation, so be an adult.

Be Assertive

Relationships with early adolescents must happen within structure. This means establishing limits and exercising discipline (which we'll discuss further in chapter 11). As I discovered at the camp, enforcing the rules did not diminish my standing with those boys. My fellow counselor, the junior high teacher, knew that. In fact, the opposite seemed to be true—being firm and even being stern enhanced the relationships.

Good parents know that they have to set rules and enforce them. It would be irresponsible to allow children to do anything they felt like doing. Good junior high teachers know this, and they insist on conformity in the classroom and halls.

Early adolescents need structure. Left on their own, without limits or enforcement, many go wild (as I experienced at Outdoor Education with my first attempt at maintaining order). Regardless of what they might say at the moment, I think that subconsciously they know that rules protect them from themselves and that left on their own, they would self-destruct. You can't love junior highers without disciplining them.

This means setting boundaries for your activities and meetings, stating clearly the rules and the consequences for breaking them, enforcing those rules and carrying out necessary punishments.

Be clear, fair and firm. Discipline, limits and rules will only hurt a relationship if they are inconsistent, unfair or enforced in anger. Let the kids know that you still accept and affirm them, but that their *behavior* is unacceptable. Then make them endure the consequences of their actions.

Don't let your young people walk all over you. Be assertive, and set limits. Kids will respect you for it.

Be Available

In a world of instant coffee, microwave dinners, instant access to the Web, immediate answers and simple solutions, it's easy to think that *anything* can happen quickly—almost instantaneously—if we only have the right formula. Unfortunately, such is not the case. Relationships don't happen quickly. They develop slowly over time—not that you have to be with someone *constantly* to become a friend, but you have to spend some time together and then be nearby or at least available.

Somebody has to be there
When the crowds have scattered
And the speaker
Has rushed away to catch a plane
To another city.
To another crowd.
Somebody has to be there
To pick up the ones who are left.
The ones who are strangers
The misfits. Square pegs
Being shoved by a sensible world
Into round holes.
Somebody has to be there
To comfort the awkward ones
Who have been loved
To death on Sunday
And left to die on Monday
While the personalities
Flit about in a circle
Of acceptance,

Never guessing at the loneliness
Of strangers.
—Lydia I. Carlson, Naperville, Illinois[1]

Todd was my neighbor. I had known him for about five years. When he began sixth grade, he started coming to our junior high club. Todd and I had a good relationship, not because we had done so much together, but because he had known me for a while. I was in his world, and I was available to him. Craig, however, lived on the other side of the subdivision. I would see him at school and in the neighborhood riding his bike. He also came to JV a couple of times. Our relationship began to develop because Craig knew who I was, saw me often and knew that I cared about him. Jon is another story altogether. He and I have attended the same church for several years, so I've watched him grow up. We have never been strangers, but I still have to work at relating to him, now that he is an adolescent and in the youth group.

Spending time with junior high kids means attending the choir concert, watching volleyball practice, shooting baskets with a few of them at the park or taking a group of them out for pizza after the game.

This is another area where junior highers differ greatly from older youth. When I worked with high schoolers, I would often take a guy out for a Coke to talk things over. Junior highers don't respond well to the individual approach. In fact, they may feel quite uncomfortable one-on-one, not knowing what to talk about. It would be better to spend time with a small group of friends. There will be opportunities for talking individually with these young people, but the relationship building will be more effective at activities or with small groups.

Don't think you can walk into a group and immediately have their friendship. Schedule time to be with kids, getting to know them and letting them know you.

Be Active

The best way to get to know junior highers is through activities, by doing things together. Go out for ice cream, ride bikes, go shopping, take in a ball game, play computer games, watch a movie—the list is almost endless. Junior highers are filled with energy, they want to have fun, and they want to be good at something (see chapter 2). Maybe that's why our church Mystery Trips are so popular. Whether it's bowling or baseball, kids get involved and bring their friends. Find out what they're interested in and offer to do it with them. In the process, you'll win their respect and friendship.

Friendships are also an important part of involvement. Special activities like camping or overnight trips allow a cohesive bond to grow within a group of kids. Loyalties develop, and kids are more likely to become involved in the program itself because they feel comfortable. They feel that they are part of the group. Participation becomes more than going along and being a spectator. Friendship and love draw them into the group, as well as their love and respect for the leader, who encourages them to be part of the group. The program is not as attractive to the kids as is the friendship of the group and the love for their leaders. —E. G. von Trutzschler, "Youth Ministry Is More Than a Meeting"[2]

Be Affirming

Everyone wants to be known and to be noticed, especially by people important to them. This goes double for junior highers. Make a point of learning names, greeting kids by name and offering sincere compliments.

"Hi, Lisa," my wife said as we walked into the sanctuary. "It's good to see you today. We missed you last Sunday. By the way, that's a pretty dress."

"Thank you," Lisa answered. She smiled and joined her parents in the row ahead of us. Lisa and her family have just started attending our church. Gail has tried to make her feel welcome.

Some time ago we had a visitor in Sunday School. At first she didn't want to join us because she didn't know anyone. I assured her that she would fit right in. Then I asked her name. She said she didn't want to tell me because everyone would make fun of it. I said we wouldn't. "Morgan," she whispered. "My name is Morgan."

"That's a great name," I said, and I introduced her to the rest of the class. They had overheard my assurances to her about her name, so they were polite. During the class, this girl actually volunteered to read a few of the verses aloud. Afterward I thanked her for reading.

Look for ways to affirm the Lisas and Morgans in your life. You may have heard that Jeff won an award at school, that Dana made the volleyball team or that Jimmy's project was in the science fair. Go out of your way to congratulate them. It will show that you care. Look through the paper for names and pictures of kids you know. Clip out the picture and mail it with a brief note. They'll love it!

Of course, we shouldn't expect kids to always respond positively to our affirmations. They may simply mumble or mutter and walk away. But we should keep at it—eventually it will make a difference.

Martin Luther King, Jr., once observed that we can change only those we love. Without affirmation, neither families nor individuals can be encouraged to discard harmful attitudes and behaviors and to pursue proper growth. Youth ministers are always building on the positive—and that positive is often discovered only through time and creative relationships. —Dean Borgman, *When Kumbaya Is Not Enough: A Practical Theology for Youth Ministry*[3]

Be Aware

Although early adolescents will not talk much about their feelings or about intellectual issues, teachable moments will occur. You never know when they will ask a serious question or want to talk, so you always have to be sensitive and ready to respond at the right time.

- Trudy's grandmother is quite sick.
- Liz didn't make the basketball team.
- Jerome's parents are getting a divorce.
- Bill says he is an atheist.
- Julio asks why there's so much pain and suffering in the world.
- Francine says she's disgusted by the way kids treat each other at school.
- Wade wonders about evolution.

As you spend time with young people, even the craziest kids will have serious moments or times when they are open to serious thoughts. It would be great if we could predict when those moments will occur, but we can't. So we always have to be ready "to give an answer" (1 Peter 3:15).

Hints and Warnings

Don't Misread Body Language
In a long meeting, young people will be restless. It doesn't mean they don't like you or the program; their bodies just have to move. In a church service, they may look incredibly bored, leaning back, slumped to one side or leaning forward with head in hand. Of course they may be bored, but that doesn't mean they are against Christianity. And often they just don't know what to do with their arms or legs.

Don't Embarrass or Make Fun of Them
Remember, these young people are trying to feel good about themselves, and they fear looking bad in front of their friends. Give them the chance to succeed in your activities and then praise them for it. Watch out for games that make them look foolish. This is also true for reading and praying aloud. Ask for volunteers or choose those who have volunteered previously. Or ask ahead of time if they want to read or pray aloud.

Contact New Kids Through Friends or at Your Activities

Remember, parents and school administrators are very suspicious of adults who hang around kids. When you go to the school and it's not a public occasion, let the principal know why you are there.

Keep Track of Your Contact with Individuals

Each time you have a memorable time with someone, jot it down on a file card or in a notebook. Keep a record of each young person, listing prayer requests, interests, goals, etc. Also record your observations of the person and your relationship with him or her. This will help ensure against spending all your time with a few people and missing others. At team meetings, you and your fellow youth workers can compare notes and pray for special needs.

 What surprises me is that our most pivotal experiences have nothing to do with skits, discussion starters, crowd-breakers, films or small-group discussion techniques. It seems that the years have taught us what ministry is really about: what God does inside kids, inside us. Not the external stuff, but the internal stuff. Not big changes, but small, gradual transformations. —Mike Yaconelli, quoted in "The Bests, the Worsts, the Firsts"[4]

The key to effective ministry with young people is relationships, getting to know young people personally and letting them know you. With junior highers, this happens by being adult, assertive, available, active, affirming and aware. Then you will be able to cross this relational bridge with Christ's love.

Ministering to Junior High Girls

Foundation 1: Have an awareness of the differences between boys and girls.

Foundation 2: Realize the special needs of girls in this age group.

Foundation 3: Design a strategy to meet those needs.

Differences	Needs	Strategy
Physical: • Develop ahead of boys • Concerned about appearance	• To accept the changes	• Activities that don't change appearance • Nonathletic event can be boys vs. girls; otherwise mix teams
Social: • More serious conversation • Big-group oriented • Aggressively pursue boys • Verbal distracters	• To talk • To be part of group • To develop relational competency • To express self verbally (boys distract physically)	• Balance activities with discussion time • Don't single them out • Reinforce appropriate behavior • Use peer pressure for discipline
Mental: • Grasp concepts more quickly	• To be challenged	• Explore possibility of outside input
Emotional: • Life is "tragic" • Emotional ups and downs	• To gain perspective on personal situations • To understand that the changes are normal	• Develop simple action plans for situational problems • Meetings should take into account these ups and downs

—Laura Laffoon and Dr. Carla Waterman, *Campus Life/JV Newsletter* [5]

Think It Through

1. If you were starting a junior high ministry from scratch, besides school, where would you meet kids?

2. Considering your (and their) schedule, when would be the best time for you to spend time with kids?

3. Think of the junior high young people you know. What are they interested in? What activities do they enjoy?

4. Considering the interests of your kids, your schedule and the resources of the community, what activities could you do with small groups of junior highers?

5. As a ministry team, what might be your strategy for building relationships with young people?

Chapter Seven

Getting Through

This chapter is about evangelism, bringing the young person to the gospel or bringing the gospel to the young person. As we discussed in chapter 3, it is possible to manipulate children emotionally to get them to make a decision for Christ. But that would be irresponsible, and I doubt that those decisions would be genuine.

On the other hand, if we believe the Bible, we know the necessity of making a personal commitment to Christ, and we feel the urgency of communicating that message and challenging people to respond. It's a matter of life and death—of heaven or hell.

My point is that we must responsibly and lovingly confront young people with the claims of Christ and call them to commitment to Him. But it won't be easy. In fact, it will seem like the following maze, with barriers at every turn. We may think we're making progress, and then *bam!*—we hit a wall. In order to know how to respond to these barriers, let's examine each one of them.

Barriers

1. Has short attention span	7. Lacks Bible knowledge
2. Preoccupied with self	8. Pressured by peers
3. Easily distracted	9. Doesn't want to be known as "religious"
4. Difficult family life	10. Has misconceptions about life
5. Doesn't think conceptually	11. Thinks church is boring
6. Not thinking seriously	12. Has misconceptions about God

Communication Barriers

Short Attention Span

Talking to a group of junior highers can be a frustrating, difficult task. Their minds wander, and their hands move continually. But consider the young person's plight. It's not easy keeping that growing body still and quiet for very long. Like having shaken up an open bottle of Pepsi with your thumb on the top, the energy is just waiting to be released. So don't be surprised if your young people fidget, talk, poke their neighbors or throw things during your careful explanation of the four spiritual laws. After all, they have to do *something* with those arms and legs.

The class is going well, I thought as I wrapped up the lesson, telling the Bible story with dramatic flair. For the past few minutes, every junior higher in the class had been quiet and seemed to be listening to everything I had to say. Suddenly Brian's hand shot up, and I thought, *Something I said must have hit home! This will be a good chance to see how much he's understood.*

"Yes, Brian?" I motioned for him to speak.

"What time is it?" he began. "Last week you let us out late."

After regaining my composure—and the class—I made the final point and closed in prayer, wondering if *anything* had gotten through that Sunday.

Preoccupation with Self

Remember when you were talking with a friend but not really listening because you were thinking of a pressing problem or concern? After an embarrassing pause, you had to answer, "I'm sorry—what did you say?" It's difficult to concentrate when your mind is somewhere else. The same is true of junior highers.

Kids in this age group are preoccupied with themselves: their looks, performance, feelings, abilities and so forth. Boys worry about what to wear to school and when their voices will change. Girls spend hours fixing their hair—watch a group of junior high girls walk by a mirror or a store window. And remember for older students especially, this is when they begin to notice the opposite sex. You may be talking about commitment, but they may be thinking about cosmetics.

Distractions

No matter what you're talking about, when something catches the eyes or ears of junior highers, it captures their attention—the toilet flushing upstairs when you meet in the basement, the dog in the back of the family room, the car squealing its tires around the corner or even a casual reference in your talk.

In one Sunday School class, I used a movie as an example. Suddenly three or four boys were talking about the movies they had seen recently. In the same class, Andrea interrupted one of my meaningful monologues to ask if she could go to the bathroom. In a youth group meeting at someone's home, I forgot to remove the younger sibling's box of stuffed animals from the room. When I turned my back, they became missiles hurled by boys sitting near the box. Potential distractions are limitless.

Family Tensions

Let's face it, the American family is in trouble. For years we have heard of rising divorce statistics and the growing number of single-parent families. Add to this the revelations of physical, sexual and emotional abuse, and we begin to wonder how any child can escape unscarred. Of course, it's not all bad—most families offer security and nurturing. But don't assume that your group is immune to those problems and tragic situations, especially if you work with a cross section of kids in the neighborhood.

Even in the *best* families, there are normal stresses and strains—between husband and wife and between parent and child. Frayed nerves, disobedience, accusations, arguments, groundings and other common household tensions will tend to clutter students' minds and emotions. They will find it difficult to concentrate on your words when they are recovering from a conflict at home.

Concrete, Not Conceptual, Thinking

Scripture is filled with profound, life-changing concepts. Volumes have been written on faith, grace, atonement, justification, redemption, incarnation, sanctification, inspiration and other deep theological verities. But early adolescents are not thinking conceptually. If the truth is not explained in concrete terms they can understand, they will turn you off quicker than you can say "substitutionary."

Many young adolescents attend our junior high groups who appear normal and healthy, certainly not abused in any way—yet they may suffer from a lack of support, guidance, and encouragement in the home that will ultimately scar them more severely than physical violence. It's this kind of abuse that's difficult to detect, yet our churches are full of well-meaning parents who, in this way and for whatever reason, abuse their children by default. They are too busy or too tired to spend time with their kids, so they expect someone else to do it for them. —Wayne Rice, "Focus on Junior High"[1]

Few Serious Thoughts

This does not mean that junior highers think only about things that are humorous. But seldom do they think about the deeper issues of life, such as meaning, purpose and the future. One reason for this we have just discussed—junior highers don't think conceptually. But it is also due to their lack of experience and perspective. Up to this point, life has been relatively simple and comfortable for them—their shelter, food and clothing have been provided by others. And life is exciting as they learn about themselves and the world. Ask a man turning 40 to reflect on the meaning of life, and he will have much to say, often through tears. But that question would be nonsense to a child who is just beginning. This is a difficult barrier to overcome, because there's nothing more serious than the gospel.

Lack of Bible Knowledge

The gap between the evangelical world and the world at large is growing. Despite the explosion of Christian media, music and literature, society is becoming increasingly secular. Most children, therefore, have little or no religious background, especially in the Bible. Even kids who have grown up in the Church seem to know very little about God's Word. "Gospel," "apostle," "Philippians" (not to mention "Habakkuk"), "disciple," "Pharisee," "Messiah," "prophet," "cross" and "resurrection" are foreign words to them. So when you read or refer to a Bible passage, chances are your young people won't be able to put it into context to fully appreciate its meaning.

Peer Pressure

Junior highers are very sensitive to what their friends are thinking and doing. They will cluster and choose a best friend. And the loss of that best friend can be traumatic. Kids can also be cruel with their words—taunting, making fun and cutting down others. In addition, every group has an unspoken pecking order, even at church. The leader sets the pace, and the others follow. Obviously, then, what certain kids think is very important to junior highers. Seldom will they respond individually and openly without regard to what others may think or say.

Aversion to a Religious Reputation

This goes along with the peer-pressure barrier. Many young people begin pulling away from church during the junior high years. And most of their school friends aren't very involved in church. One girl was called "church lady" by a group of boys because she was involved in our youth group. She hadn't been pushy, condescending or pious, but they mocked her faith. Adults will often do what is right, even if it costs friendships. But young people fear rejection by their peers and will shun anything that might give them a goody-two-shoes reputation.

Misconceptions About Life

As previously mentioned, early adolescents have experienced very little life in their 11, 12 or 13 short years. To them, pain is the exception and pleasure is the rule. And *now* is all that counts—5 or 10 years is an eternity. In addition, they believe that everything revolves around them, their needs and schedules. These and other misconceptions come with being young, but they will be a barrier to any serious discussion of sacrifice, the future, commitment and selfless service.

Misconceptions About Church

Many kids see church as boring and irrelevant. The music is slow and dull, the Bible seems old and out-of-date, and the sermon is long and incomprehensible. They would much rather sit in the back with their friends and pass notes than participate in the service. Instead, they have to sit uncomfortably with the family. Of course, considering their needs and the other barriers described earlier, many of the church programs probably *are* boring and irrelevant. But this idea about church can carry over to any church program. They think, *If the church sponsors it, I won't like it.* So they resist going or, if they do go, they resist listening to what is said.

Misconceptions About God

Young people also often harbor strange mental pictures of God. To many He's an old man, hopelessly out of touch with the world today.

To some, He's a stern judge, waiting to stop anyone from having fun. To others, God is a great disappointment—they blame Him for physical problems, family situations or personal tragedies. Those without any church background may form their ideas about God and religion from the caricatures on television and in the movies. And to some, God is simply a concept, impersonal and unknowable. A misconception about God will stand in the way when you are trying to convince a person to give his or her life to Christ.

These barriers can be formidable for anyone trying to tell early adolescents about Christ. But effectively communicating the gospel to junior highers is *not* an unreachable goal. The barriers are not impossible to overcome. There *are* communication principles that will help you surmount the obstacles.

Communication Principles

Build a Base
Professional baseball is a fascinating game to watch if you appreciate the athletic skills needed to play the game and know the strategies involved on the field.

The count is two and two. As the pitcher begins to release the ball, the runner on first breaks to second. Because the batter is left-handed, the shortstop moves to cover second base to take the throw from the catcher. But the batter slaps the ball between second and third for a hit, in the space vacated by the shortstop, sending the runner to third. The play is called a hit and run, and it's beautiful to watch when executed properly.

Now let's suppose that I am the manager of a Little League team. Having studied the game for years, I decide to teach my young athletes the hit and run. I would be wasting my time. Instead, I should teach them how to hit and how to run. Only when they've mastered the basics will they be able to move on to more complicated plays.

Teach When Opportunities Arise

These are teaching moments in the traditional sense. When a child goofs up, you can teach that it's not the end of the world. When he achieves something special, you can reinforce how his hard work paid off. When she loses a friend, you can share about how disappointing life—and friends—can be at times.

Opportunities don't have a good sense of timing, so you must be on the lookout at all times. From articles in the newspaper to graffiti on the bathroom wall at school, opportunites to reinforce your values abound if you will only keep your eyes and ears open. —Bill Sanders, *Seize the Moment, Not Your Teen*[2]

Or suppose you want to learn a foreign language. In your first class, the teacher gives you a lesson with complicated sentence structure and technical vocabulary. And your assignment is to read a chapter of a book in this new language. That would be ludicrous, because first you must learn the rudimentary aspects of the language.

Now consider your group of early adolescents. How will you explain incarnation, atonement and salvation to them? Unless you build a base of knowledge so that they will know what you're talking about, you will be wasting your time. This is especially true for the unchurched; they know nothing about the Bible and very little about Jesus. Another term for this process is "preevangelism." Simply stated, it means setting the stage for evangelism, preparing the way for effective communication of the gospel.

Of course, each person and each group are unique. So the first step will be to take a close look at your kids to determine how much they know about God, Jesus and the Bible. When in doubt, assume that they know very little. Regardless of the group, here are some guidelines to follow:

- Know where you are going with your teaching. In other words, remember that you are laying a foundation for a purpose—to build on it and eventually share the good news.
- The basics of the gospel are the person of Christ, the reality and consequences of sin and the necessity for a personal faith commitment. Decide when and how you will explain these basics. Don't just tell Bible stories that lead nowhere. Have reasons for teaching what you do.

Where Do You Do Evangelism?

There are two aspects to our evangelistic thrust. During the regular meetings where we talk about life skills, our goal will be pre-evangelism, setting the stage for an evangelistic appeal. We will be giving young people Bible content by using biblical illustrations as we teach life skills. Each of these weekly meetings will have near the end a one-point message where we give a simple teaching from Scripture. Again this is pre-evangelism. This is helping kids who are scripturally illiterate learn more about Jesus and have a basis on which to make a decision. The main evangelistic thrust, however, will be at the big events. The speaker at these events will give a clear Gospel presentation and invite the young people to respond. A three- to four-week small group will be initiated during which the Gospel will be explained clearly and concisely with a question-and-answer time. The young people will be challenged to accept Christ as their personal Savior. —Dave Veerman, *Campus Life/JV Newsletter* [3]

- Use stories from the Bible to illustrate points in your other teaching. For example, if you want to tell your group members how to make friends, you could use Jesus' discussion with the woman at the well as an example of how to start a conversation. Although that's not the point of John 4:1-26, telling that story will teach students something about Jesus as they see Him in action. These illustrations will help build their Bible knowledge.
- Center on Christ. Let your young people know that Jesus is both God and man. As a man, He struggled with the same temptations and pressures that they experience. They will be able to identify with a real, historical person.
- Keep your talks short and to the point, keeping in mind the limited attention span of your audience. It is best to have *one* point for each talk. For example, you could tell your class about when Jesus returned to Nazareth and was rejected by his former neighbors and friends. Your point could be that Jesus knew what it was like to be misunderstood and rejected.
- Use literature, news events, movies, videos, contemporary music and other resources to reinforce what you are teaching.
- Make the Bible available. Give away Gospel portions or New Testaments of an easy-to-read version like the *New Living Translation*. Then provide a reading plan with the Bible divided into bite-sized chunks.

Before young people can make a personal commitment to Christ, they have to know who He is. Building a knowledge base means letting them know that Jesus is fully God and fully man; born as a baby in a manger, He came to Earth to show us what God is like and to die in our place for all the wrong things we have done; He was tempted just like us but never gave in; He was killed, executed like a criminal by being nailed to a cross; He rose from the dead and is alive today. Of course, just knowing those facts doesn't make someone a Christian, but it's a start.

Focus on the Truth

Although it is tempting to pull emotional strings to get young people to respond, don't do it. Instead, emphasize the *facts* of the gospel story. Kids must know that they should follow Christ, because He is *truth* and His message is *true,* not because they will get something in return.

People play bargaining games with God: "If You get me out of this mess, I'll be good." Such games betray a very immature outlook on God and life, but junior highers are very susceptible to it. They may pray for good grades or to win games, wear a cross for good luck, or accept Christ to bring Mom and Dad back together. So don't encourage following Jesus for selfish reasons.

An effective method of communicating with high school and college young people begins with addressing their felt needs. Talking about loneliness, self-concept, fear, sexuality and so forth will get their attention and open the door to the gospel. But this approach is usually not very effective with junior highers. They are concentrating on competence, not identity, and their emotions fluctuate greatly. A felt need one moment may be forgotten the next. Lay a factual foundation for commitment to Christ.

When you present the facts of the gospel, let your young people know that the Christian life isn't all fun and games. In fact, it may involve hardship and difficulties. God does not promise to take us *out* of our problems but *through* them (see John 16:33).

Also let your group members know that they can't depend on anyone else's faith. They are growing up and must make their own decisions. In other words, no matter how little or how much they know about God or have gone to church, each person must make his or her own decision about whether or not to follow Him.

Near the end of summer after eighth grade, Kara reported to the church about her experience at camp. As a proud father I heard her say, "I was worried about starting high school this fall, thinking that kids might call me a 'Jesus freak.' But then I thought, *That's what I am*, and so why should I worry about what they say?" Then she asked the congregation to pray for her during the year.

Kara's decision to live for Christ at school was based on her commitment to Christ—the truth—and not on emotion or the prospect of personal gain. It was a significant step in her growth as a Christian.

We follow Christ because the gospel is *true*, and Christ is the only way (see John 14:6). Give your young people the facts.

There are three major phases in effectively communicating the Gospel to junior high students.

Contact is where we meet kids. This may happen at lunch, at a sporting event, or at a roller skating rink. First impressions are important because junior highers judge immediately. Staff members' love for the Lord and for young people must be real and show through their lives in the first contact.

Conduct is the key. The staff person's life in front of the young person will be one of the first times the Gospel is communicated to him or her. A junior high school student will take notice of an adult who actually lives differently from the world's standards. As this staff person "fleshes out" the Gospel, the student will be curious about what makes him or her tick. Overwhelmed by the simple joy, love, and faith of the staff, the student will want to find out more.

Content is the handle. The student sees the staff person living the Christian life, but he or she will need words to help him or her understand. The words of the Gospel do exactly that—they give him the verbal handles to the non-verbal actions of the staff. —Greg Johnson, former editor of *Breakaway* (Focus on the Family's junior high boys' magazine)[4]

Use Words They Understand

You are a well-educated adult who spends most of your time speaking to other adults about adult concerns. Undoubtedly your vocabulary reflects your maturity and education, as it should. But the vocabulary of most early adolescents is very limited. Remember, some of them only learned to read five or six years ago. Few read books on their own. And even those who are voracious readers often skip over difficult words—very few would even know what "voracious" mean.

In the mid-'80s, when I decided to dive into the age of information and buy a computer, I had a terrible case of computerphobia, intimidated both by the technology and terminology. As I ventured from store to store, the salespeople seemed to be speaking a foreign language—I didn't even know what "hardware" and "software" meant, not to mention "RAM," "DOS" and "bytes." I'm sure that the salespeople wanted to convince me to buy a computer, but they rattled on in computerese, and I was totally confused. Each time I would nod and utter a few "hmmms," as though I understood, and then make my escape as quickly as possible. It wasn't until I read an article in *Consumer Reports* magazine and had a friend explain what everything meant in words I could understand that I overcame my fear and returned to the computer marketplace. If I hadn't been so highly motivated, I might never have bought one.

In the same way, our adult words and Christian clichés can be very intimidating to young people—and they aren't nearly as motivated about Christianity as I was about computers. Remember this when you teach, especially when you come to words such as "grace," "mercy," "faith" and "sin." Use different words, or explain what each word means and give relevant examples. Then see if students can define a term in their own words or give you another example of what it means. Encourage everyone to ask questions, especially when they don't understand a word, term or phrase. Effective communication means using language that your listeners understand.

Don't Just Speak to the Group

Individual communication is vital with this age group because of the great differences that can exist in one group. There is a vast difference between the typical sixth-grade boy and typical eighth-grade girl. These differences not only include physical size but also social skills and the ability to think.

Keep Saying It

Don't assume that because you have covered a topic once, it has been heard, understood and applied. You may have to repeat some truths over and over until your young people catch on. Some of the barriers described earlier may have kept a person from understanding what you were saying the first three times you said it. But the fourth time, the light goes on, and the young person responds.

This doesn't mean that you should always tell the gospel story the same way. Use your imagination and creativity. A young person may respond to a visiting speaker or a personal testimony even though he has heard you give the same message several times. God may use the fresh voice, a different illustration or a new slant to get through.

Also keep in mind that your junior highers just may not be ready to respond. Salvation is a work of the Holy Spirit, not a response to a clever sales pitch. We must faithfully and responsibly present the message, but God will do the convincing.

During the summer, churches from a number of communities joined together to sponsor a series of evangelistic meetings. The advertised programs featured outstanding music, comedy, testimonies and a well-known speaker. We took our group on youth night. The kids stomped, cheered and clapped to the music, and they laughed hysterically at the comedian's routine. Impressed by the program, I could hardly wait for the speaker, thinking he must be terrific. But I was really disappointed. Although articulate and funny, he seemed to ramble on and on and cover the same territory over and over. And our kids seemed to lose interest; they started talking, passing notes and making frequent trips to the bathrooms. You can imagine my shock when, during the invitation, one of our boys went forward—he hadn't seemed to be paying attention at all. But God used something the speaker said to break through, and Drew gave his life to Christ that night.

Present the message clearly and simply, and keep saying it. Be patient—and keep praying for those who have not yet responded.

Provide Opportunities to Respond

Beyond presenting the message of Christ, you must also provide opportunities for young people to respond, without putting them under great pressure (trying to manipulate them emotionally) or embarrassing them.

 Following my high school Bible study a few weeks ago, I was talking to one of our adult sponsors who had been a missionary overseas. I was telling her that sometimes I feel guilty for not being a missionary to another culture. She shot back, "You are a missionary to a different culture. These high school kids"—she pointed to a few kids who were still left after the youth group meeting—"live in a different world. You've chosen to infiltrate that world to give them the message of Jesus." —Jim Burns, *The Youth Builder* [5]

This may be done very naturally on an individual basis. If you have built a relationship with a young person, you can simply ask him or her what he or she thought about the talk, about what you have been presenting all year or about Christ. You could do this after one of the meetings. Or you could explain to the whole group that you want to meet with each person individually, just to see how they're doing. Then no one will feel singled out. (Make this announcement light or humorous, so they won't dread the interview.)

Response cards can also be an effective method for setting up personal appointments. After a meeting, give everyone an index card and ask them to answer a question about the meeting. The question could be as simple as "What are your suggestions for future programs?" or as serious as "From what you learned tonight, what is Jesus like?" Then explain that you or another member of the staff would love to get together with anyone personally to explain more about how to become a Christian, a true follower of Christ. Explain that those who want to get together with you should write their names on the bottom of the cards and then you or someone on your staff will contact them in a day or two. Then collect all the cards. It is important that everyone receives a card and writes something so that no one will feel singled out. Response cards can also be effective in large group meetings where the speaker can ask for reactions to the message.

Another effective opportunity for response is to invite kids to become involved in a small group where you will discuss how to become a Christian. This group could meet for four weeks, covering one main point of the gospel at each meeting. The method you use isn't the issue; the important thing is to give kids the chance to respond to Christ's call.

Be Prepared to Share

You should be ready to take advantage of opportunities that arise as you spend time with kids. Teachable moments often happen when you least expect them, so always be sensitive to the Holy Spirit's leading and be ready to respond. This is not to say that you should unload the whole gospel story each time someone comes to you with a problem, but you should be sensitive to opportunities to share about Christ.

- Marlene sees your Bible in the car and says something about "not being able to understand that book."
- Scott declares that he doesn't believe in all that "God stuff," because he's never seen God.
- Toni wonders about some preacher she heard about on the news.
- Estelle says she went to church once with her grand-mother, a long time ago, but hasn't been back since.
- Brent asks a question about prayer.
- Philip is visibly upset over his parents' impending divorce.

God will give you opportunities to share the good news. Be ready.

Learning to Understand Them

Good junior high workers understand junior high students. They are able to identify with early adolescents; they can empathize. Most adults can't. To most adults junior highers are beyond their understanding. They can't understand why junior highers are so moody, noisy, angry, disrespectful, irreverent, smart-mouthed, and lazy. All of these behaviors may be true about particular junior highers, but usually there are good reasons for them. What junior highers want from adults is someone who looks beyond their behavior and tries to understand. Without this understanding, communication becomes almost impossible. —Wayne Rice, *Junior High Ministry* [6]

Be Prepared to Lead

You should also be prepared to lead a young person to Christ. Evangelism is not just presenting the whats, whys and hows of the gospel—it is also personally introducing young people to Christ. Be sure to think through the process, what you will tell the person and how you will pray.

Here's a quick summary of what I do. After explaining *how* to become a Christian (the process), I usually pray first, aloud, thanking God for this special young person and asking Him to give the person the courage and faith to make his or her commitment. Next I have the person pray aloud, expressing sorrow for sin and gratitude for what Jesus did on the cross and then asking God to come in and take over his or her life. Then I pray aloud again, thanking God for what He has just done in this person's life. Afterward, I ask the person to explain what just happened, and I encourage him or her to tell a Christian friend about his or her new relationship with Christ.

Be prepared to share the good news and lead kids to Christ.

Be Prepared to Follow Through

Remember, accepting Christ as Savior is just the first step in the Christian walk; therefore, it is important to plug new believers into a program that will help them grow in the faith. This may mean getting them involved in a small group, giving them a workbook to finish, meeting with them regularly or some combination of these ideas. The point is to have a plan.

Follow through also means communicating with parents and helping kids adjust at home. If the young person comes from a Christian home, Mom and Dad will probably be very supportive of their son's or daughter's decision. Work with them and make discipleship a team effort.

If, however, the young person comes from a non-Christian home, you will need to help him or her translate the experience into words that his or her parents will understand. Encourage the person to *live* for Christ at home, instead of walking in the door and making an announcement.

Follow through should also involve the Church. Give young people opportunities to participate in the larger body of believers. If they don't go to your church, encourage them to get involved in one, while respecting the wishes of their parents.

Be prepared to share the message, to lead young people to Christ and to follow through.

The Key

If you tried to follow the maze at the beginning of this chapter, you found that there was no way through. Every route on the paper was blocked. That wasn't a mistake. I designed the maze that way to illustrate the fact that on our own we can't break through and bring a young person to Christ. In fact, the solution to the maze is to *go over* it, not *through*—and that means *prayer*.

Enlist the prayer support of fellow believers. And pray as a ministry team

- for individuals;
- for programs and activities;
- for opportunities to share;
- for wisdom to overcome communication barriers;
- for sensitivity to individuals and opportunities;
- for spiritual power; and
- for faithfulness to God's Word and to responsible evangelism.

You'd better have a deep love for these young people. If you don't they will see through you so fast! Do junior high ministry because you love junior high students. If junior high ministry is your step to bigger and better things, please do yourself, your church and the precious junior high students a big favor and get out. —Scott Pederson, Director of Student Ministries, Willow Creek Community Church, South Barrington, Illinois

Satan will do all he can to hinder communication of the gospel. And he has weapons at his disposal in addition to the barriers outlined at the beginning of the chapter. But Satan is no match for God. Bathe your ministry in prayer.

Whether you minister in the neighborhood or in church, you will meet junior high kids who do not know Christ. They need to give their lives to Him—it's a matter of life and death. Of course, these young people must be handled with care, but they are not too young to follow Christ. Make responsible evangelism a part of your ministry plan.

Think It Through

1. What barriers tend to keep the junior highers you know from listening to the gospel or to a lesson from God's Word?

2. Think of the junior high kids in your life. What do they need to know about themselves, God and Jesus to give them a good base for making a personal commitment to Christ?

3. Translate the phrase "accept Christ as your personal Savior" into words that junior highers could understand.

4. Besides speaking to them, what other methods could you use to communicate the gospel to a group of early adolescents?

5. Suppose a young person asked you to lead him or her to Christ. What would you do?

6. What resources do you have for following through with new believers?

Chapter Eight

Getting Together

They just kept coming—Mary and two friends, Carol, Tommy and his neighbor, Linda, Justine, Craig, James—each one greeted warmly by members of the ministry team. Soon, 50 (normal attendance was in the 20s) eager and enthusiastic young people packed the room, laughing and talking among themselves. Jeff stepped to the front and, as though on cue, the crowed quieted to hear his opening comments.

Jeff welcomed everyone, described the first game and divided the group into teams. Kids quickly organized and then cheered as teammates passed shaving cream from nose to nose. The next crowd breaker was a spirited bubblegum race, seeing who could be the first to blow and pop a three-inch bubble. Then the group searched for unique items in an indoor scavenger hunt.

After quieting everyone, Jeff introduced the slide presentation, a study in loneliness. The lights dimmed, and the projector flashed a series of somber images with a blues song serving as background. Then, turning on the lights again, Jeff asked for the group's reaction and led a lively discussion on life's lonely moments.

With the discussion setting the stage, Jeff wrapped up by explaining how Christ could be their friend and bring them through their lonely times. Then he distributed index cards so that they could register their reactions and indicate whether they wanted to have a personal appointment with a staff member.

After collecting the cards and pencils Jeff thanked the group for coming and sent them to refreshments. Quickly flipping through the react cards, he saw that six kids had indicated their desire to know more about Christ.

What a meeting! thought Jeff . . . then he woke up.

Most youth leaders dream of such a meeting, where attendance is great, the projector works, kids are attentive, everything goes right and everyone responds positively. But usually that's just a dream. In fact, many meetings resemble nightmares instead.

Jeff was expecting 20 kids but 10 (and no one else from the ministry team) straggled in and sat at the edges of the room, talking loudly among themselves. Carol was reading and laughing over notes that Todd had written to Justine, and Tommy was picking dirt out of the bottoms of his Nikes (the dirt pile was almost as high as the shoe). After three unsuccessful tries, Jeff finally got the group's attention and over loud objections divided them into two teams. The first game quickly deteriorated into a shaving cream fight until the cans were confiscated. As for the bubblegum race, no one was able to blow a bubble, so it was declared a draw. The scavenger hunt began well but soon became chaotic when everyone began charging to the front with each item.

Jeff decided to move to the slides, but he soon discovered that no one was watching. Mercifully, the bulb burned out. The discussion and wrap-up followed suit, with Jeff spending most of his energy trying to get everyone quiet. And when he distributed index cards, handmade airplanes filled the air as he searched for pencils. Finally, in disgust, Jeff dismissed the meeting and watched everyone stampede to the refreshment table.

Meetings and special events can be valuable ministry tools, providing a place for finding fun, friends, food and faith. But good meetings don't happen automatically. They take good planning and proper execution.

Meeting Plans

The Objective
As we discussed in chapter 3, the first step in creating effective meetings is planning, and a good plan begins with an objective. In other words, you should think though the purpose of the meeting, what you want it to accomplish, and then write out your objective.

The Purpose of Programs

Programs are tools that we use to make junior high ministry possible. It's important to remember that they are not ends in themselves. They simply provide opportunities to do ministry—to be with kids, to talk with kids, to laugh and play with kids, to share Christ with kids. Programs are the disposable part of youth ministry. It's best to "use 'em and lose 'em." It's always dangerous to let programs determine what the ministry will look like. It's the ministry that should instead determine what the programs look like. —Wayne Rice, *Junior High Ministry*[1]

Obviously, effective meetings can help you achieve the goals of your youth ministry. Specifically, they can help in four different ways.

1. They can build a sense of identity and unity, giving kids a place to belong.
2. They can provide an accepting atmosphere, allowing kids to speak their minds and to be themselves.
3. They can offer good, clean fun.
4. They can communicate biblical content.

The first three are accomplished in the *way* the event is run, including the setting and atmosphere. Numbers 1 and 2 will govern how you welcome kids and make them feel at home, and they will determine the ground rules for how you expect kids to treat each other. Number 3 will affect your choice of activities and how you run them. In essence, those three goals are usually beneath the surface, unspoken. But they should be considered when planning any event.

Number 4, however, is the most important one to consider when writing your objective statement. What do you want kids to know or do as a result of the event? If your goal is evangelism, you could write "As a result of this meeting, kids will know what it means to become a Christian and will be given the opportunity to respond." If your meeting is about family relationships, your objective could read "As a result of this meeting, kids will express love for their parents by writing thank-you letters to them."

If you have a clear and concise objective, the meeting will be easy to plan as you evaluate each part of the meeting in light of that objective.

The Timing

Next you should think through the timing of the event—*backwards*. Decide when you want the meeting to end and make sure you have time for the most important parts. The whole meeting should be designed to meet your objective, but certain ingredients are more important than others for effective communication. Many times I have attended large rallies where a well-known speaker was flown in at great expense. As a trained and experienced professional, this speaker was hired to bring a gospel challenge. But the program was so cluttered with music, skits, announcements and games that by the time he or she was introduced, everyone was ready to go home. Too often we get so carried away with our games and creativity that there is no time for the heart of the meeting.

It is also important to use program ingredients that enhance, not detract from, the message. Don't expect kids to go bananas one second and listen quietly the next. Think about how you can set up the speaker or teacher and make communication more effective. Whatever you use to communicate the content, make sure that the rest of the meeting flows toward it. Good timing is critical.

The Response

It's also important to think through how you want kids to respond, what you want them to do. Will you give them an assignment to carry out during the week? Do you want them to talk with staff? Will you ask them to fill out a react card? Will you have them pray? Of course, how you want the group to respond will be directly related to your meeting objective.

Meeting Principles

As you design your meeting, be sure to remember the principles described here; they apply to any junior high event.

Youth group activities are a positive alternative to an often negative social environment. Young people have a critical need to develop strong, healthy social relationships. And entertaining social events can be just as important as spiritual and academic training.

Entertaining activities help kids learn how to play. Fierce competition and structured athletics have hurt kids' ability to create their own fun. Good social programming can teach teenagers the power of positive partying. They can learn how to have a good time without drugs, sex, or alcohol. —Scott Noon, "Are You an Entertainer or a Minister?"[2]

Make the Meeting Active

Because junior highers are so filled with energy, they will not sit still for long periods of time. Instead of fighting their energy, take advantage of it by employing active games that you can control and by not having them sit very long for any part of the meeting.

Early adolescents' energy can be a blessing or a curse. They can have fun with almost anything you do. In fact, two junior high boys will chase themselves all over the lawn at any given moment. So you don't have to plan complicated and sophisticated activities to entertain them. At the same time, however, their energy can destroy a meeting if you're not careful. So let them get some of the energy out of their systems, but don't let them get out of control.

Move the Meeting Along

Because these young people have such short attention spans, divide your meeting into five- to seven-minute segments. This can be done even in a Bible study. You could begin by using games that are discussion starters and then break into small groups for answering questions about Scripture. This could be followed with a quiz, in a game-show format, on the information just learned. Then kids could apply the lesson by analyzing case studies. You could conclude the meeting with a challenge and prayer.

Each program should also have a tight structure with no gaps between elements. Move quickly and smoothly from one part into the next.

Keep Everything Simple

This principle applies to the whole event and to each part. The procedures and rules of your games should be easy to explain, and the meeting should move in a straight line toward achieving the objective. Explain the meeting to a friend. If he or she seems confused, so will your junior highers; so simplify it.

Taper the Meeting

This relates to the timing of the meeting as described earlier. Schedule your more active and loud games first; then follow with ones that are a little less involved. This will help with crowd control and will allow you to get your group's attention for serious communication.

In the meeting described at the opening of this chapter, Jeff's slide show was preceded by an indoor scavenger hunt. What a mistake! After running around the room and cheering loudly, it's almost impossible for junior highers to suddenly get quiet and serious, especially with the lights off.

Allow Time for Socializing

Junior highers are just discovering what it means to be social, and they want to talk to each other. Provide time for this, before the meeting and afterward. One church's youth group meetings are scheduled to begin at 6:30 P.M. and end at 8:00 P.M. The meetings themselves last only about 45 minutes, beginning at 6:45 P.M. and ending at 7:30 P.M. Afterward, there are refreshments. Kids can socialize during the 15 minutes before, as everyone arrives, and the half hour after, during refreshments.

Social events will also help meet this need. That's one of the reasons we have special events and mystery trips for our church youth group. They offer opportunities for fun and for being with friends.

Acknowledge Social Differences Between Junior High and Senior High Students

When working with youth, it is vital that we not assume that all age groups are the same and can be treated the same way. Simply stated, an 11-year-old girl and an 18-year-old boy are two extremely different people. There are drastic changes that occur during the teenage years, so we must keep in mind the differences.

1. The junior high student is more interested in anti-social acts just to see what will happen. Generally, the high school student knows and has deliberately chosen to do a certain act.
2. The junior high student is extremely critical and often unkind in his remarks. The high school student has more manners and a higher regard for the feelings of others.
3. Junior high students tend to form their own cliques more than high school students.
4. Junior high students are still trying to find themselves, while high school students are farther down the road physically and emotionally.

Build Excitement in Programs
Excitement is based on the following factors:

- A past history of excitement (it'll snowball)
- Music playing as your young people enter the room
- What you say as you open the meeting
- The type of crowd breaker that you begin with (a big opener!)
- How you explain the instructions (be enthusiastic)
- The time limits
- Giving everyone the chance to move around
- Music playing as the crowd breaker is happening
- The progression of the crowd breakers
- Group members seeing themselves in slides or videos

- How much group members' friends are part of the meeting
- Your attitude ("I'm gonna have fun!")
- How well you publicize and psyche up your kids for future activities
- How you relate to the other staff during the meeting
- How well you're heard
- Doing the unexpected
- Playing on school spirit
- Lighting, room temperature, decorations (posters and banners)

Think Through Every Aspect

The idea here is to anticipate potential problems so that you can prevent them. Ask yourself what could possibly go wrong with each meeting element, and think how your kids might respond. This analysis should also include the setting, staff, equipment and props. Is there enough room for everyone? What kind of distractions could there be? What will you do with the broken balloon pieces? Where will you store the props until you need them? How will you set up the projector and screen so that they won't be in the way during the rest of the meeting? Who will get the refreshments ready, and when will they do it? How can you be sure the room temperature is comfortable?

A few years ago we held our Campus Life/JV Float Soak (the kick-off event featuring free root-beer floats) in the lower gym at the school. The room was used for wrestling and broom hockey and had a cement floor. Besides being uncomfortable, the room was very noisy. In addition, some of the boys brought their skateboards. You can imagine our crowd control problems. I could have saved myself a lot of grief if I had checked out the room ahead of time and had foreseen the potential problems.

Taking time to think through and think ahead will help you run a smooth and effective program.

Keep These Tips in Mind

- Don't use paper. Some kids will crumple it or make it into paper planes immediately. Instead, use index cards or larger pieces of card stock.
- Pick up all props immediately after using them. Kids will find ingenious alternate uses for them.
- Make sure all the games are fair. Every kid thinks he or she is a lawyer and will accuse you and the other team of cheating if he or she is losing.
- Watch out for lopsided scores. This will deflate any contest. You could stop the game early and declare the winner; then start a new game, giving the losing team another opportunity (you may want to reorganize the teams at this time). Or you could use creative scoring, awarding double points later in the game.
- Keep soft drinks cold and then serve them in cups, without ice. Cubes usually find their way down others' backs, and cans get sprayed around the room.
- Get to the meeting place early to arrange the room the way you want it.

Meeting Parts

We've discussed meeting plans and meeting principles; now let's take a look at some specific meeting ingredients.

Crowd Breakers

As the name implies, the main purpose of crowd breakers is to break down social barriers, help kids get to know each other, and build the group. Crowd breakers can include competitive games, group tasks, songs—just about anything that involves everyone and is fun. These activities don't have to be tied to the theme of the meeting, but they should help you achieve your objective. For example, their main purpose may just be to establish the right atmosphere for communication.

When choosing or creating crowd breakers, you should be able to answer in the positive seven key questions.

1. Will this be fun?

Your group may participate because you ask them, but ideally you want them to enjoy what they're doing. Kids should look forward to this time of the meeting. Picture yourself in their place and ask yourself, *If I were in junior high and with this group, would I enjoy doing this?*

2. Will this be fun for everyone?

Don't use crowd breakers that favor the bigger and stronger kids, making the smaller ones losers or leaving them on the sidelines. Choose nondiscriminatory activities. Games with blindfolds and unusual rules can put everyone on the same level. And in group tasks, everyone works together to accomplish a goal.

Don't choose activities that only a few kids appreciate. Sometimes quizzes fall into this category. A few kids may enjoy them while everyone else is bored. Of course, everyone doesn't have to actively participate to be involved. You can have contests with two or three competitors at the front of the room while the rest of the crowd watches, laughs and cheers.

3. Will this affirm kids?

Beware of anything that may embarrass individuals. With growing and often awkward bodies, fragile egos and glaring social needs, junior highers need to be built up, not torn down. Use crowd breakers to give them opportunities to succeed, not fail. This doesn't mean that everyone will win every game—in any competition, someone has to lose. But instead of treating them as losers, treat them as runners-up and compliment them on trying and on doing well, even though they didn't win.

This whole area of competition should be handled with care. Competition can be healthy and can motivate the group to participate and succeed—if the competition is kept in check. If you use teams, *don't* let the kids choose or divide up on their own. Instead, consider the easiest way to divide the kids so that the teams are evenly matched. You could have one half of the room against the other, boys against girls, sixth and seventh graders against eighth graders (if the numbers are equal) and so forth. Or you could just place kids where you want them. If these teams will be competing in a series of events, award points for every place so that no team is blown out. Last Sunday, for example, we began youth group with a series of competitions between two teams. In each game, the winning team received 2,000 points and the other team 1,000.

Don't, however, make winning a big deal by making a grand announcement and awarding a super prize. We usually just acknowledge the winning team or let them get in line first for refreshments. These kids want to win, but they really aren't that concerned about being the grand champions of all time. In fact, at one of our Campus Life/JV area events, we formed new teams for every contest: by schools, birthdays, ages, color of clothing, etc. Everyone still competed hard in every game.

4.   Will this be easy to explain, run and control?
As mentioned earlier, everything in the meeting should be as simple as possible. Lengthy and complicated explanations will lose most of the kids; numerous props will be broken, lost or used as missiles; chaotic or wild games will destroy the meeting.

At one event, I had a game where each person was supposed to have five balloons tied to his or her arms and legs. You can imagine what happened as I distributed strings and balloons to the crowd of 75. No one understood what to do, and they began popping each others' balloons as soon as they were inflated. Then they began chasing each other around the room. I had to quickly confiscate all the props and move on to another game.

One of the great things about junior highers is that they are easy to entertain. You don't have to have complicated and creative crowd breakers to get them involved. At a recent youth group, the guys asked if they could play tag in the field before we began. And they are always asking to repeat popular crowd breakers from other meetings.

Keep everything simple.

5. Will this facilitate communication?

In other words, will this crowd breaker move the group *toward* or *away* from the goals you want to accomplish? Everyone may love a shaving-cream fight, but I doubt that it would help you study the Bible together. Keep the meeting objective in mind as you choose the crowd breakers.

6. Will this model the right values?

Nothing in your meetings should contradict the values and priorities you are teaching. Don't do anything that could go in a different direction. Often team leaders are more competitive than the kids. This is especially true for younger leaders who often will do almost anything to help their teams win. I have seen youth directors argue with referees in basketball games and cheat at volleyball. What messages do those actions communicate? On the other hand, think about how leaders could turn losing into winning by encouraging and affirming team members, playing fair and having good attitudes. Make sure that the staff understands whose needs are being met.

And stay away from all sexual innuendoes and bathroom humor. Junior highers are notorious for talking gross, so you can get easy laughs with certain jokes or comments. But that's the wrong direction. Don't do it and don't allow it. How you run the games, how you treat kids and how you talk and act will say much about you and your values.

The Content of Your Meetings

1. Focus on early adolescent relationships rather than issues. If you deal with the issues that arise out of their relationships (friends, authority figures, parents, etc.), you will find young people more readily able to put the concepts into practice in their lives.

2. When planning the content of your meetings, do not assume that these young people know a lot of facts and related material, including Bible content. Do not assume that they understand basic truths or basic principles. They may be able to repeat the principles but have no idea what they really mean.

3. Gear your content to the maturity levels that are evident in your group. Junior highers can range in maturity from very, very childish to quite adult acting and sophisticated. —Sandy Jones, former Junior High Club Director, Central Florida Youth for Christ[3]

7. What are the strengths of the meeting place and how can I use them?

Take advantage of your environment—don't fight it. If the weather is good, go outside for the first part of the meeting. Every setting can be used for crowd breakers. A park may have playground equipment, pinecones, insects, trees and athletic fields. A church may have a piano, chalkboards, folding chairs, hymnals and Sunday School supplies. A family room may have children's toys, a Ping-Pong table, a VCR, easy access to a kitchen and old clothes. Take advantage of what you have.

Although you will use more games in some meetings than in others, try to have at least one crowd breaker in every meeting, even in Sunday School. There, you could open with a contest that would help you review what you have covered (for example, Wheel of Fortune, Hangman, Who Wants to Be a Millionaire, scrambled words from memory verses, etc.) or introduce the topic of the day through activities such as collages, lists or songs. You could end your class with another game *if* you have time (this can serve as an incentive for your young people to help you get through the lesson). For one quarter, we ended each Sunday School class with a Bible drill, boys against the girls. The kids loved it! I thought it was old, but they had never done it before.

Other Discussion Starters

In addition to crowd breakers and games, other group activities can help prepare the group for discussion, Bible study or a wrap-up. These include simulation games, role-plays, group reactions, instant dramas, and pictures. Videos can be very effective, especially if you stop the tape in the middle of the story and discuss with your group what has happened and what they think will happen next. Just be sure to preview all videos before you show them.

Young people seem to be obsessed with music. Use this to your advantage in the meetings. Play a popular song and ask what a certain phrase means. Or talk about the kinds of values the singers portray through their lifestyles.

I have found that junior highers love to be in the spotlight, on stage. Again, capitalize on this interest. Beforehand, choose kids to act out a special minidrama or role-play in front of the whole group. This can be an effective way to focus on typical situations at school or at home, to bring Bible stories to life or to solve typical interpersonal problems. Be sure to choose the right kids for these plays, and give them an opportunity to rehearse or to think about what they will say. Otherwise you may have someone just stand at the front and giggle.

The Difference the Differences Make

The differences between junior and senior high students create a chasm. The latter see sixth graders through eighth graders as emotionally immature, socially uncool, intellectually shallow, and generally not with it. Junior highers often feel socially snubbed, intellectually outwitted, and physically outdone by the older kids. A separate, unique program is necessary to reach junior high students.

Careful attention should be made to keep the junior high program distinctly different from the high school program. To some extent this will occur naturally as we attempt to meet their needs, but it is important that activities and games that are traditionally used in high school ministry are not used here. After two or three years in a junior high program, students should move on to something new and fresh in high school. —Greg Johnson, former editor of *Breakaway* (Focus on the Family's junior high boys' magazine)[4]

Discussions

Whether or not it is possible to have effective discussions with junior highers depends a lot on the ages of the kids in the group and their intellectual development. Some will enjoy talking about biblical themes, felt needs and life. Many, however, will become quickly bored with discussions of any depth.

Discussions can help kids get involved in meetings and think through issues if they are handled correctly. Here are some guidelines for effective discussions.

Concrete, Focused and Life-Related Issues

If you ask what grace means to them, you will be met with silence. But if you ask for examples of how teachers are unfair at school, you will get an earful.

One very effective discussion starter is to use case studies of other junior high kids. You could say, "At church, Kenny learned that as a Christian, he should be loving and kind to others. The next day, Monday, he was walking down the hall at school when he saw Barry being picked on by some older boys. They were knocking his books out of his hands and making fun of him. What should Kenny do?" After they respond, ask, "What would you do?"

Or you could say, "Mary is having a tough time in math. Her teacher, Mr. Reed, seems to always pick on her. He won't let her do extra credit to improve her grade, and once he even accused her of cheating when she wasn't. What should Mary do?" Then ask, "What would you do?"

Kids will discuss issues related to their lives and situations in which they can identify with the kids in the story.

Excellent resources for case studies include the *Student's Life Application Bible* and *Sticky Situations* by Betsy Schmitt (see "For Junior Highers" in the resources section of this book).

A Moving Target

This is a time of rapid change—young people are not only changing in themselves from week to week, but no two junior highers will experience this changing in the same way. Programs aimed at the needs of a particular age group may or may not hit a junior higher, simply because he's a moving target. We need to make sure our programs and activities vary sufficiently to give junior highers the individual attention they need. —Wayne Rice, "Focus on Junior High"[5]

Short Questions That Have Short Answers

Such questions can help you focus on a specific Bible passage. To review Luke 4:16-30, you could ask, "How did the people in Jesus' hometown treat him? Why? How did Jesus respond to what they did?"

What you don't want to do is ask such a question as "What happened when Jesus returned to His hometown?" That's a little too long and open-ended.

I must quickly add, however, that you should avoid yes-or-no questions. The answers to such questions are short, but they require very little thinking. One Sunday I overheard a junior high teacher attempt to lead a discussion by asking, "When the disciples saw what happened, they didn't like it, did they?" ("No.") "Do you think Jesus knew that would happen?" ("Yes.") "That's right. And He knows what will happen in our lives too, doesn't He?" ("Yes.") "Have you ever felt like the disciples?" (Silence and a mumbled yes.)

If a question is worth asking, usually it can be stated in a way that would avoid a simple yes or no answer. For example, the last question the well-meaning Sunday School teacher asked could have been rephrased as "When have you felt like the disciples, angry and confused?"

Here's another tip if you are in a church setting. Don't ask questions that can be answered with the usual Sunday School answers: "Jesus," "God" or "the Bible." From their earliest years, children who grow up in church learn that those answers are usually right for almost every question they're asked.

Questions That Move You in the Right Direction

Instead of one large question, think of a series of smaller ones that get the discussion started in the right direction. Let's say that your topic is how to improve relationships with parents. Instead of asking, "What can you do to improve relationships at home?" you could ask, "What kinds of things do you and your parents usually fight about? How do those arguments usually end? Who wins? Let's take that one area of cleaning your room. What might you do to stop an argument about that before it happens?"

Groups of Five to Seven People

The goal of a good discussion is to get everyone involved. In a large group, this is impossible—either everyone will be talking at once or most of the group will lose interest while a few discuss the issue. By breaking into smaller groups, each with an adult leader, you will be able to get participation from almost everyone. Of course, this will mean that you will have to prepare ahead of time with your staff, giving them the questions to ask in the groups. If you reassemble as a large group for reports, have the adult leaders give quick, concise summaries of what each group discussed and decided.

Dividing into groups will also help you with crowd control. One junior high Sunday School class I know of is organized around four tables. Each table has five kids and a leader. In another church with a very large junior high attendance at Sunday School, the group is broken down into many classes.

Clear Ground Rules

Let everyone know what is acceptable and unacceptable behavior during your discussions. Here are some examples:

- Only one person may speak at a time.
- You may speak only when the leader recognizes you after you have raised your hand.
- No gross talk or swearing is allowed.
- No cutting down others is allowed.
- Be quiet and listen when someone else is talking.

Come to an agreement on your rules and write them out as a contract. Let your students give their input on the rules.

Also, during a discussion, you should act as moderator and facilitator and not give your opinions on the answers or take sides. Never condemn or comment negatively on an answer—you'll lose the students. This doesn't mean you shouldn't challenge a wild or weird statement or bring the discussion back on track. But try to be neutral and to accept each young person's answer. After the meeting you can tell them what you think or show them what the Bible says. Use discussions to get kids thinking about important issues and to set the stage for communication.

What Our Lives Preach

Our activities mean more than just good, clean fun. They provide action models of the Christian life. In an activity with students, our actions will speak very loudly. Here we can demonstrate mature Christian values and attitudes. If we cheat while playing a game of football with the students and then during the meeting tell them about the importance of being honest, they will be more likely to remember our actions, not our words. On the other hand, if we play fairly and do not lose our cool when we drop a pass or blow a play, the students will see our attitudes and want to imitate them. Remember, we are models. Many of the students are patterning their lives after us. When honesty is discussed in the meeting, the students will have a better understanding of its importance because they have just seen it demonstrated in football. —Greg Johnson, former editor of *Breakaway* (Focus on the Family's junior high boys' magazine)[6]

Bible Studies

Some of your meetings will center on the Bible. It is important that your young people know God's Word, what it teaches and how to study it (we will discuss this in more depth in chapter 10). Here are some guidelines for incorporating Bible study into your meetings.

- Use an understandable translation of the Bible and make sure everyone has a copy.
- Help students find their way around the Bible (most don't know the books of the Bible).
- Don't embarrass poor readers by surprising them and having them read aloud. Give your readers time to practice before the meeting.
- Study one story or paragraph at a time. In other words, keep the lesson short and simple—don't try to cover the whole Old Testament in one quarter.
- Put the passage in its historical and cultural setting. As I've mentioned before, most kids, even church kids, know very little about the Bible or have any sense of history.
- Find the biblical principles—the timeless truths—in each passage and show how those principles apply to the lives of young people today.
- Help students design action plans to put the lessons into practice.

Wrap-Ups

Talking to junior highers can be intimidating. But there comes a time when someone has to summarize, teach and challenge—in other words, speak to them. How can you keep the attention of a restless group of adolescents who are probably uncomfortable and thinking of refreshments? Then, how can you connect, communicating God's life-changing message?

It's not easy. Don't assume that because they like you or because you're the leader, kids will pay attention. Often they can't help themselves from moving around or talking with friends. But you *can* get through.

Of course, your task will be much easier if the rest of the meeting has been designed properly, so the students will be prepared to hear what you have to say. But even if everything has gone perfectly and your young people are quiet and ready to listen, you have to be careful or you will lose them. As you prepare and deliver your talk, remember that there are several key components in a successful wrap-up.

One Point (Two at the Most)

Don't unload the whole counsel of God in one talk. Decide on the most important truth you want to communicate and then concentrate on that. Cover the next step or additional truths in future meetings.

Object Lessons or Case Studies

The more concrete examples you can use, the better. When talking about peer pressure, I will often bring a balloon and show how it reacts to being squeezed from one side and then the other. It gives in and bulges out the other side. ("Sometimes we feel like that, don't we?") Eventually it pops under pressure from all sides. Then I bring out a basketball and try the same kinds of external pressures. The point is that we need the strength on the inside to withstand the pressures from the outside.

All around us there are objects that we can use: a nail (crucifixion of Christ), a cocoon (new life), a leaf or flower (the wonders of creation), a flashlight (direction, guidance), books, dirt, pictures, bicycle spokes, computer disk, string, eraser, etc. Use your imagination.

Case studies and true-life examples will also be effective. Look for news stories about young people. Or write your own case studies. Young people enjoy stories. Whether it's a fable or the story of a junior high student in another town, they will listen if you tell it well. Your own testimony also fits into this category.

Brevity

Don't ramble on, making the same point over and over in one talk. Think in terms of speaking for five to seven minutes. Only if you are an experienced speaker who knows how to keep junior highers' attention through humor, illustrations and stories, should you go longer. Your talk should wrap up what has already happened in the meeting, as opposed to being sermon length and introducing three new points.

A Personal Tone

Avoid preaching at these kids. Instead talk with them. Don't demand their attention because you are in charge. Gain their attention because of who you are—someone who cares about them—and because of what you have to say.

Response Time

Whether you are presenting a Bible lesson or an evangelistic challenge, it is important to give kids a chance to respond, to put into action what they have learned. Use reaction cards, questionnaires, assignments, raised hands, appointment cards or some other method to reinforce your teaching.

Because junior highers love to get together and to have fun, meetings and other events can be key elements in the ministry. To have dream meetings instead of nightmares, plan carefully—assemble the parts and remember the principles—to meet your objectives.

Veerman's Laws for Youth Meetings

1. There will always be a pet in the house that will wander into the room.
2. If there is a TV in the room, it will be turned on.
3. If something can spill, it will.
4. The projector bulb will burn out.
5. The printed announcement will always have an important typo (day, time, place).

6. Half of the kids will not know about the meeting (they didn't get the mailer or get called or see the announcement in the bulletin).

7. When you give a junior high kid a paper to keep, he'll lose it in less than 10 minutes.

8. Surefire crowd breakers always bomb.

9. When you have filled up every minute of the meeting in your planning, everything will take longer than you expected.

10. When you already have gaps in the meeting in your planning, everything will go more quickly than you expected.

Think It Through

1. What would you like to see your youth-group meetings accomplish?

2. Where will you hold these meetings? How often will you meet?

3. What advantages and disadvantages does that meeting place have?

4. How will you divide among the ministry team the responsibilities in a typical meeting?

5. What resources do you have for crowd breakers, discussion starters, discussions, Bible studies, skits, plays, videos, music and wrap-ups?

6. If you or your church has very few of those resources, where can you get them?

7. What role will kids play in planning and running the meetings?

Chapter Nine

The How-Tos

model (mád-l) n. [L *modus*, a measure] 1. a small representation of a planned or existing object 2. a person or thing regarded as a standard of excellence to be imitated 3. a style or design 4. one who poses for an artist or photographer or who is employed to display clothes by wearing them v. 1. to serve as a model 2. to represent others of the same style

role model (ról mád-l) n. a person so effective or inspiring in some social role, job, etc. as to be a model for others value (vál-yü) n. [L *valere*, be worth] 1. the worth of a thing in money or goods 2. estimated worth 3. purchasing power 4. that quality of a thing which makes it more or less desirable, useful, etc. 5. a thing or quality having intrinsic worth 6. [p.] belief of standards 7. relative duration, intensity, etc.

teach (tēch) v. 1. to show how to do something; give lessons to 2. to give lessons in (a subject) 3. to provide with knowledge, insight, etc.

skill (skil) n. 1. great ability or proficiency 2a. an art, craft, etc., especially one involving the use of the hands or body 2b. ability in such an art, etc.[1]

In chapter 3, I said that in ministering to junior highers we should model values and teach skills. Now that we've defined our terms, let's look a little closer at what it all means.

Model Values

Simply stated, a value is something of worth. Our values, therefore, are those things, qualities or beliefs that are valuable to us: possessions, people, activities, ideas, truths.

And modeling means representing or living out—providing a living demonstration. So modeling values means living out what is important to us.

Regardless of what we say, we communicate our values by how we act and react. In fact, we cannot *not* model values. Compare your reactions to a broken lightbulb and a dented automobile. Undoubtedly you would be much more upset over the car than the bulb, because the car is worth more. You value the automobile more highly.

We also demonstrate what is valuable to us by how we treat things. My computer is valuable to me, so I keep it secure, clean and covered. But I don't care that much about my old running shoes, so they lie in a corner of the garage.

In addition, we speak volumes by how we spend our time, especially in extremes. I may say that sports aren't important, but my actions will contradict my words if I spend every Sunday afternoon glued to the televised game of the day.

And we communicate our values by how we spend our money. My father-in-law was determined that his son and daughter graduate from college. He sacrificed and saved so that his dream could become a reality. Education was valuable to Dad.

All of these examples involve observable actions and reactions. Children especially are influenced by role models (parents, teachers, older kids, sports heroes, ministers and others they look up to). They take it all in—and learn.

Now think for a moment. What kind of role models would you like *your* children to have? What kind of values would you like these adults to portray? I would like my kids to see people who walk their talk, living out biblical values.

A short list of biblical values would include

- making Christ the center of our lives (Matthew 6:33);
- caring for those in need (Matthew 25:31-46);
- loving God with all our hearts (Luke 10:27);
- loving our neighbors as ourselves (Luke 10:27);
- loving our brothers and sisters in Christ (John 13:34,35);
- loving our families (Ephesians 6:1-4);
- praying (Ephesians 6:18);
- reading, studying, and applying God's Word (2 Timothy 2:15).

I'm sure you can add to this list.

As Christians and as Christian ministers, these values should be reflected in where we give our attention, how we spend our time and where we invest our resources.

My point is simply this: We who lead, teach and counsel young people wield tremendous influence by our lifestyles. Kids look up to us, and whether or not they realize it, they copy how we live. A vital part of the ministry is modeling values.

And it doesn't matter if you are only with some kids for an hour or so a week. What they see in you can still influence them. At the very least you can reinforce the positive values that others are modeling.

Treating young people with respect and love, accepting and affirming individuals, playing fair, doing the assignments that you give the class, taking an active role in church, going out of your way to see kids or to drop them notes and cards, speaking out against what you believe is wrong—all of these actions model Christian values.

But we've touched on all that before. The heart of this chapter is the last half of the phrase "model values and teach skills." So let's look at what it means to teach skills.

Teach Skills

With the dictionary's help, we have seen that a skill is a proficiency, the ability to do something well. When this term is used, doctors, musicians, craftsmen or technicians usually come to mind. If we say a surgeon is highly skilled, we mean that he or she is at the top of his or her profession. But skills are important in every area of life, and the most important of these are basic life skills.

Simply defined, a life skill is the ability to perform well a life-related task. Life skills include how to make friends, how to communicate effectively, how to be a good friend, how to make a decision, how to take care of yourself, how to solve problems, and many others.

As adults, we take most of these skills for granted, but we learned them at some time in our lives. And the time that they should be learned is in early adolescence. We have already discussed the fact that children at this age are working on developing competency (see chapter 2). They want to be able to do things adequately, to accomplish something, to be good, to learn how to. At the same time, they are in transition physically, emotionally, intellectually, spiritually and socially. They are moving toward becoming independent and living on their own in the world, so they desperately need to learn how to relate and how to function in society.

Parents and others often assume that children will learn life skills by watching moms and dads in action—that these skills can be caught through modeling. But as important as modeling is for inculcating values, it doesn't work for learning skills. Skills must be taught.

Consider, for example, a young boy and his shoelaces. He can watch someone tie his shoes day after day, for weeks. By watching, he will know that tying shoes is important. And as he trips over his own laces, he will learn that tying them is important to him. But he still won't know *how* to do it himself until he is taught.

We should train junior highers in the basic skills that they'll need for adulthood. Emerging adults need to learn how to make good decisions, how to take responsibility, and how to communicate with others. In the past, adolescents became apprentices to adults who taught them the skills that prepared them for adulthood. Today the only skills many adolescents learn are playing video games, watching television, listening to rock music, and surviving on junk food. Unfortunately, these skills are of only questionable use in adulthood. —Wayne Rice "Focus on Junior High"[2]

That's a simple example—tying shoes is not a crucial skill. Eventually a child will learn from someone, or the child will wear slip-ons the rest of his or her life. There are more important life skills that should be learned. In fact, most social scientists agree that the absence of life skills can be devastating to children; and, in fact, it is one of the leading causes of delinquency and crime. They also agree that the best time to teach life skills is during early adolescence.

As we minister to junior high young people, we can help meet this pressing need. Consider teaching life skills as a part of your junior high ministry.

Teaching any skill involves four steps: explanation, demonstration, supervised practice with feedback and independent practice in a real-life setting.

According to H. Stephen Glenn and Jane Nelson, all children must develop four sets of skills in order to function as capable, self-reliant adults:

1. Strong intrapersonal skills (the ability to understand personal emotions, to use that understanding to develop self-discipline and self-control, and to learn from experience)
2. Strong interpersonal skills (the ability to work with others and to develop friendships through communication, cooperation, negotiation, sharing, empathizing, and listening)
3. Strong systemic skills (the ability to respond to the limits and consequences of everyday life with responsibility, adaptability, flexibility, and integrity)
4. Strong judgment skills (the ability to use wisdom and to evaluate situations according to appropriate values)[3]

If I were teaching you how to use an electric lawn edger, first I would explain how the edger works, pointing out the blade, guide, cord, switch and other important parts. I would also explain how to hold the edger, how to place it between the sidewalk and the lawn and how to operate it. That's explanation.

Next I would demonstrate the equipment for you. After unwrapping the extension cord and plugging it in, I would place the edger between the lawn and sidewalk. Then I would press the switch and push the edger a few feet, holding the guide against the sidewalk, while carefully explaining what is happening. Afterward I would ask if you had any questions.

In the third step, supervised practice, I would give you the tool and let you try it yourself, under my watchful eye. As you edged a few feet of lawn, I would make sure you did it right, making corrections and answering any questions you might have about the operation of the equipment.

For the final step, you would be on your own. I would give you the edger so that you could edge your own lawn. Before you left, I would encourage you to call if you needed help.

That's how to teach skills—explanation, demonstration, supervised practice and independent practice. But how does this relate to junior high ministry? Let's expand these steps to show how they would fit into a youth meeting.

Objective

What do you want students to learn? Divide the larger skill into bite-sized pieces; then write a concise and measurable goal for the meeting. For example, developing strong interpersonal skills, one important life skill, could be broken down into recognizing emotional clues, describing feelings during difficult times, identifying contributing causes for feelings and reacting to intense feelings. How to manage money could be divided into getting more money without depending on gifts, dividing money (simple budgeting), designing a spending plan, avoiding impulse buying and shopping to get the best value for the money.

As you begin to teach the skill, simply tell students what you are going to teach them. State what you would like to see happen as a result of the time together. In a meeting about avoiding smoking, drinking or drugs, you could say, "As a result of this meeting, you will choose to stay away from the power stealers—alcohol, cigarettes and drugs. Our goal is that you will choose life."

You don't always have to give the objective, but saying it helps everyone understand where the meeting is going.

Set

Why do the learners need to learn this? When you came to me and asked to borrow my lawn edger, you already knew that you had a need. You were ready to learn. Kids, however, often have no idea that they need to learn certain life skills. They may sense that something is wrong, but they will seldom identify the reason. It is important, therefore, to set the stage for the teaching by getting students ready to learn.

This can be done by explaining why the material is important, presenting the advantages of learning the material, and relating the material to life experiences at school, church or home.

A series of questions, a game, case studies, role-plays or other discussion starters can be very effective. In Set, you help students see and feel a problem so that they will want to find the solution.

Delivery

What content do I want them to learn? How will I teach this content? For this step, select the material to be taught and the appropriate teaching approach, and then teach toward your objective, using creative methods. This is the explanation step we discussed earlier. Having presented the problem in Set, you are now giving the solution.

Suppose you wanted to teach kids where to find friends—that was your objective. For Set, you could have them list the first names of all the kids they know at school. Then, looking at their cards, they could identify those on the list whom they would like to have as friends. Next you could tell them a story about a boy who just moved to a new town and had no friends. Afterward you could say that probably, at times, all of us have felt lonely, like that boy. We wanted friends but didn't know where to find them. Then you could explain that as a result of this meeting, they will know where to find potential friends.

Because of Set, your students would be ready to hear what you have to say. They would be ready for Delivery. Be creative and concise as you deliver the skill. Make the point and give them a way to remember it. I have found that acronyms work well. For example, to resolve conflicts at home, just remember CLASP: C=calm down; L=lower your voice; A=acknowledge the other person's request; S=state your request; and P=propose a solution.

Physical objects can also be effective. For the lesson on conflict resolution, we gave all the students a metal clasp to keep in their pockets as a reminder of our acronym.

Demonstration

How can I show them what I mean? Don't just talk about the skill; give concrete examples. Anyone can demonstrate the concept or skill you are trying to get across, including the leader, another volunteer or other students.

As in our edger story, this step means giving a living example of what you have just taught. Consider the lesson on resolving conflict. As the teacher, I could demonstrate CLASP by role-playing with another staff member a typical fight between siblings, working through CLASP one step at a time. Afterward I could have kids point out what I did to acknowledge his request, etc. Then we could act out another situation. It is important for students to see the skill in action.

Check

Is the content and process at the correct level of difficulty? This means making sure the learners understand the material. You can use a variety of monitoring devices such as raised hands, discussion, sharing with a neighbor or comment cards. Use Check throughout the teaching session.

Practice

How can I let them try it? Learning + Practice = Retention. Give students an opportunity to practice the skill, with immediate feedback and reinforcements. With some skills, this will be easy, because they can do everything they should right in the room. If you were teaching them how to start a conversation, they could divide into pairs and start conversations using the method you just taught them.

Some skills do not lend themselves to physical practice in a meeting (for example, finding friends, responding to a crisis, shopping, studying, etc.). But students can still practice by thinking through what they would do in certain situations by role-playing or by responding to case studies.

Whatever the skill, young people need the opportunity to practice under your supervision.

Social Competency

 One of the important components in preventing adolescent chemical abuse is social competency. A number of social skills, all of which can be promoted by family, school, church, or other organizations, can serve as important factors in prevention. These include friendship-making skills, communication skills, decision-making skills, and the ability to say "no" when peer pressure mounts. —Dr. Peter L. Benson, president of Search Institute[4]

Action

How can I help them apply this to their lives? This requires independent practice—an assignment for students to carry out during the next week.

Summarize, give opportunity for questions and comments, and then tell them what to do during the days that follow. Have kids report to someone during the week or at the beginning of your next meeting. The assignment is not complete until they report back.

Here are some examples of action assignments:

- This week, meet three new people.
- This week, check and double-check your work on every test you take at school.
- This week, do one of the actions you wrote on your card for improving your family times.
- Use one of these compliments when you get home and use all three during the week.
- This week, read the Bible for about five minutes every day.

Plan Each Meeting

As you plan each meeting for teaching life skills, remember Objective, Set, Delivery, Demonstration, Check, Practice and Action. In Youth for Christ's Campus Life/JV program, these elements are divided into eight segments.

The *Opener* (5 minutes) is a game or activity designed for fun and to help everyone relax and get into the meeting. The openers are not too rowdy but involve everyone and are active.

Announcements (5 minutes) comprise another game or creative presentation to promote upcoming events and highlight special occasions within the group (special awards, birthdays, etc.).

Starters (5 minutes) are activities designed to set the stage for the teaching, helping the young people think about the topic that will be taught. Typical starters are quizzes, role-plays, skits, case studies and stories.

Tell (5 minutes) is the delivery segment where the life skill is taught.

Show (5 minutes) is the segment where the life skill is demonstrated.

Do (10 minutes) is an activity designed to reinforce the main point of the teaching by having young people practice what they have just been taught.

Thought for the Week (5 minutes) is a Bible lesson designed to build a foundation of biblical knowledge, so students can make responsible and thoughtful decisions for Christ.

The *Biggie* (5-15 minutes) is a meeting-ending game or activity to give everyone something to look forward to and to give them something to talk about at school the next day. It usually involves competition between individuals, team representatives or small groups.

You may organize your meeting differently by adding games or music—just be sure to include the teaching elements.

Outward appearances can be deceiving. A mature looking 13-year-old may be very immature. So don't be surprised when kids act their age (or younger). You can't always tell what they're like by looking at their physical development. Too often youth workers assume that the more mature kids don't need the basics or personal attention, when, in fact, they may need it more.

This also highlights the need for a team approach to the ministry so that individual attention may be given where needed. —Dr. Richard Dunn, pastor of Leadership Formation, Fellowship Church, Knoxville, Tennessee

Besides the life skills that I listed earlier, there are other skills that Christian young people need to learn. These include how to pray, how to study the Bible, how to worship, how to serve others, how to share their faith, and so forth. Consider teaching these spiritual life skills when you design Sunday School or other Christian education programs. We will discuss how to study the Bible in the next chapter.

Because early adolescents are at the crossroads and are working on competency, they need to learn life skills. Model values and teach them skills.

(By the way, can I have my edger back?)

Life Skills Evaluation

To help students better gauge where they stand and how they can improve their life skills and, in turn, their relationship with God, adapt this evaluation[5] for use with your youth.

	Beginning	Intermediate	Advanced
	1 2	3	4 5
Prayer	Talks to God when in trouble	Prays for own self	Has a prayer list
	1 2	3	4 5
Bible Study	Reads the Bible occasionally	Knows how to have devotions	Has a regular Bible study
	1 2	3	4 5
Church Attendance	Chooses, attends and finds friends at church	Attends church & youth group regularly	Worship Sacraments Small Group
	1 2	3	4 5
Language	Before swearing, counts 10	Makes positive comments, reduces swearing	Encourages others
	1 2	3	4 5
Physical Care	No drugs Begins personal hygiene	No smoking or addictions	Improves dress, hygiene, diet, and exercise
	1 2	3	4 5
Problem Solving	Recognizes problems, chooses alternatives	Understands lordship of Christ	Uses "Stop, Look, Listen, Go" to solve problems
	1 2	3	4 5
Spiritual Growth	Recognizes areas of need	Seeks Christ's attitude; balanced life	Sets goals for personal growth
	1 2	3	4 5
Love Toward Others	Stops resenting others	Understands Golden Rule; shows kindness	Makes sacrifices for others

Think It Through

1. What values do kids see modeled by the way you teach and relate to them?

2. From your observations of junior high kids, why is it important for them to learn life skills?

3. What life skills do the kids in your youth group need to learn?

4. What program do you have in place where you could teach life skills?

5. Who would be the teacher?

6. What spiritual life skills do your kids need to learn?

Chapter Ten

Route 66

The teacher stood and read from the book:

And it came to pass, verily, that she seemeth amongst and in the midst, that he sayeth unto her, "Yea and wouldest thou that whatever he wilt shalt be done according to whowhatwhensoever Ezracharophis, begotten of Zedopariah from the land beyond Berithamah cometh?"

Insomuch as the woman knew not the messenger nor his wondrous companions shining all about the company, and yet she remaineth silent, looking for the sign nor the seal betwixt the eyes. And the whole of the congregation around the candlestick riseth with loud praisulations according to the prophetic word (Hesitations 14:37-40).

If you found that incomprehensible, consider your poor junior highers. That's how the Bible sounds to many of them—a string of adult words and empty gibberish.

For the unchurched, the Bible is just an old book. There may be one at home, on a shelf or coffee table, but it is seldom opened. Most have very little idea of what is inside the dusty covers, although they may have heard the Bible read or quoted occasionally. For the most part, they are biblically illiterate.

Even kids who have grown up in church aren't sure what the Bible teaches. Some may know certain facts or some of the classic Bible stories, but they probably don't have the slightest idea how the stories relate to today and to their lives.

All Scripture is inspired by God and is useful to teach us what is true and to make us realize what is wrong in our lives. It straightens us out and teaches us to do what is right. It is God's way of preparing us in every way, fully equipped for every good thing God wants us to do (2 Timothy 3:16,17, *NLT*).

The Bible is God's Word, and kids need to know what it says and teaches. As people concerned about junior highers, we must teach them this most important, invaluable life skill—how to study the Bible.

Practicing What We Preach

Before we teach them, however, we should be students of the Word ourselves. This means being disciplined in our Bible study habits—reading, understanding and applying Scripture.

Do you really believe that the Bible is God's inspired Word? If so, you will read the Bible.

Do you really believe that biblical principles are relevant for today? If so, you will study the Bible.

Do you really believe that God speaks to us through His Word? If so, you will apply the Bible to your life.

Do you really believe that God knows what is best for you? If so, you will obey what He tells you through the Bible.

Take an honest look at your own Bible-study habits before challenging others to read Scripture and trying to teach them how.

Setting the Stage

One of the mistakes often made by Christian youth workers is to jump right in with a spiritual agenda, assuming that young people want to learn about God. Most kids are more concerned with grades, physical changes, social pressures and feelings of failure. And besides, why should they be interested in this ancient, dry and difficult book?

Before teaching, we must set the stage for learning.

Create Thirst

A thirsty person will readily accept an offer of a drink. In fact, he will do almost anything to satisfy his need. Unlike thirst for water, however, Bible reading is not a felt need. In fact, most kids at this age think they are doing fine on their own, without the Bible. So we must create a thirst—motivate them. We want kids to *want* to read, understand and apply God's Word. How you create this thirst, of course, will depend on the makeup of your group. Strangers to Christianity should be handled differently from VBS veterans.

Use biblical examples in your teaching and conversation

We covered this briefly in chapter 7. No matter what the subject, you can probably find a Bible story or quote to illustrate your point. Here are some examples of subjects and Bible stories that can be easily tied together.

- **Running away**—Jonah's attempt to run away from God's will and the consequence of running from the problem only to find a bigger one (Jonah)
- **Loneliness and depression**—Joseph's strong feelings of loneliness and depression when his own brothers sold him into slavery (Genesis 37:12-36)
- **Loyalty**—Ruth's loyalty when she left her homeland, friends and family and went with her mother-in-law, of all people (Ruth)

By hearing stories like these, kids will build their biblical knowledge and their curiosity. They will want to read more about the exciting characters and learn more about what's in the Book.

Don't carry this to an extreme, but sprinkling your teaching and conversation with Bible stories and examples, in a natural way, will help create interest in reading the Bible.

Give examples of how you and others have applied God's Word
Again, this can be very effective, but it must be natural, not forced.

Imagine you are talking with a few kids about summer vacation plans. You mention the fact that during family devotions (a regular time of reading and discussing the Bible), you read a verse that helped you make a decision. This casual comment can plant the thought that the Bible is a source of guidance.

Or while explaining how you coped with a personal tragedy, you share how certain verses meant so much during that difficult time. Kids would begin to see that the Bible can be a source of comfort.

Or during a discussion about love, you tell them about 1 Corinthians 13. They would start to understand that the Bible can be a source of answers for their questions about life.

When kids see what the Bible does for you, they will want to know more about it for themselves.

Use physical reminders

Schoolteachers often pepper their walls with quotes, pictures and posters, so your kids won't find it unusual for you to put a Bible verse on the wall. Christian bookstores have a fine selection of beautiful posters with Scripture references or whole verses printed on them. You can also play Christian-music CDs from time to time. And, of course, you can have your Bible with you in the car and in the room.

These visual and audio statements can reinforce the fact that the Bible is important to you and should be important to them as well.

Provide Tools

If possible, whenever you read the Bible with kids, whether it's in Sunday School, at youth group or on a retreat, make sure that everyone has access to a copy of what you are reading.

In a small group, you can have Bibles for everyone. When the Reach Out edition of *The Living Bible* first came out, I had a box of them in my trunk. Although our Campus Life Insight meetings featured discussions on Christian growth and Bible study, most of the kids didn't own Bibles; if they did, they would forget to bring them. So they would use the ones I brought. No one felt out of place, and everyone could participate. Even now, in our Sunday School program, we will bring several of the church Bibles to the classroom. Although all the students in that class own several Bibles, they usually forget to bring them to church.

In larger groups, students could pair up, or you could use an overhead projector and put the passage on the screen.

It is also important to use an understandable translation of the Bible. Don't allow archaic or adult words to become a barrier. There are several fine versions available.

As is true regarding so much of their faith, teenagers are confused about what to believe regarding the Bible. On the one hand, six out of ten (61%) say that the Bible is totally accurate in all of its teachings. They perceive its content to be valid, too: nine out of ten teens deny that anyone who relies upon the Bible for moral guidance is foolish. They accept many of the fundamental teachings contained in the Scriptures. . . .

But teens' views of Scripture are corrupted in other ways. Three-quarters believe that a core message of the Bible is that God helps those who help themselves. . . . . There is ample confusion about whether or not the Bible provides insight into moral truth and, if it does, whether such truth is absolute or relative in nature. Nearly six out of ten teens even agree that all religious faiths teach equally valid truths. —George Barna, *Third Millennium Teens*[1]

Remove Barriers

Some people avoid the Bible because it looks and feels strange to them. That's not surprising, considering the fact that the Bible is organized like no other book they've ever seen—with 66 smaller books, hundreds of chapters and thousands of numbered verses. And most kids don't know the order of the Bible books. Imagine what they think when asked to turn to Titus or Haggai.

One way to remove this barrier would be to have everyone use the same edition of the Bible and give page numbers when you refer to specific passages. You could post on the wall (on a piece of poster board) a list of all 66 books. This would also help them learn the order.

Another barrier to Bible reading is knowing where to read. Often I've heard of people who, after deciding to read the Bible, approach it like any other book and begin reading at page one. They usually stop somewhere in Leviticus. Even those who decide to start with the New

Testament get bogged down in the Gospels while reading the same story over and over.

Kids need guidance in reading the Bible, especially on their own. Mark is a good place to start. It's short, action-packed and tells the story of Jesus. James is also good, because the lessons are obvious and practical. Or you could give them a series of passages to read on an interesting subject such as love, family, the future, Satan, friends, etc.

Don't let any of these barriers stand between your young people and the Bible.

Dispel Fears

Junior highers aren't afraid of the Bible itself, but they are deathly afraid of being embarrassed in front of their peers. Many have trouble reading, especially reading aloud. They can imagine nothing more embarrassing than to stumble over a word and have everyone laugh. I'm not saying you should never have kids read aloud in your meetings. On the contrary—this can be an affirming and confidence-bolstering experience if handled correctly.

For reading the Bible in a group, you can dispel kids' fears by

- preparing them for reading aloud—print out the passages you want them to read and give them time to practice;
- setting them up for success—explain to the class that it's not easy to read the Bible aloud because of the small print and difficult words, but they should do the best they can;
- allowing no one to ridicule anyone else;
- affirming kids after they read—compliment them and thank them for helping;
- allowing them to decline—simply explain that each person can read a couple of verses (along the rows or around the circle), but they can decline if they don't want to read at this time;

· allowing them to stop and ask how to pronounce any
    word.

We can set the stage for Bible teaching by creating thirst, providing
tools, removing barriers and dispelling fears.

Choosing Curriculum

When choosing curriculum for your junior highers (or for any other
group in your church), ask the following questions:

1. Is it consistent with our goals? (Make sure it takes
   kids in the direction you want.)
2. Is it realistic? (Watch out for any material that pur-
   ports to take kids through the Bible in a month,
   bring instant maturity, develop deep disciples or
   some other fantastic claim.)
3. Is it simple, volunteer friendly? In other words, can
   teachers prepare and teach the lessons easily without
   using most of their preparation time trying to figure
   them out and collecting props?
4. Is it focused? (Beware of material that goes in three
   or four directions at the same time.)
5. Is it active? (You don't want kids just sitting and listening to the teacher talk.)
6. Is it varied and balanced?

Don't be fooled by the creative advertisements, neat packages, inexpensive price tags or bells and whistles. Open it up and read through
actual lesson plans to choose curriculum that is right for you and your
group.

Teaching Them How

Most Bible study methods have three main steps: read, understand and apply. Readers are told to answer these questions about a passage: "What does it say?" "What does it mean?" and "How do I apply it?" But early adolescents need these steps simplified and explained in concrete terms.

It is also important to start small—choose a paragraph or short story to read and study, not a whole chapter or book.

And kids need to see how the Bible is up-to-date and practical, so use contemporary illustrations and applications.

I have found a five-step Bible-study process to be quite effective. The steps are easy to teach and remember. What's more important, they answer the questions "So what?" (what does that passage have to do with me?) and "Now what?" (what should I do about it?). Use this process to teach the Bible and *teach* this process to your kids so that they will be able to study the Bible for themselves.

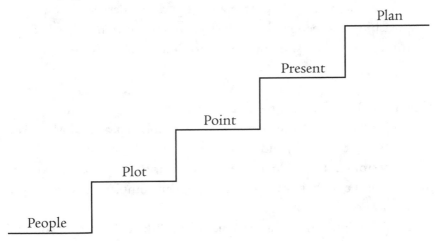

When you teach this Bible study method, don't give it to them all at once. Instead, help them master one step at a time. Because each step builds on the previous ones, you will be able to review them as you go along.

Also be sure to use many junior high illustrations for each step, especially the Present and Plan steps.

Let's consider these steps, one at a time.

People

The first step in reading and understanding a Bible passage is to identify the people involved. This is a good first step for junior highers, because it is easy and concrete. Later it will help them see themselves in the story.

The people can be those who are mentioned by name or role, those who are hearing the story, the storyteller or writer and anyone else connected with the passage.

Mark 1:1-4 (*NLT*) says:

Here begins the Good News about Jesus the Messiah, the Son of God. In the book of the prophet Isaiah, God said, "Look, I am sending my messenger before you, and he will prepare your way. He is a voice shouting in the wilderness: 'Prepare a pathway for the Lord's coming! Make a straight road for him!'" This messenger was John the Baptist. He lived in the wilderness and was preaching that people should be baptized to show that they had turned from their sins and turned to God to be forgiven.

A complete list of the people in this story would include Jesus, Isaiah, God, John the Baptist, the people who heard John speak and Mark, the writer. As you can see, by including the writer and the readers or listeners, every story in the Bible has people to identify. This is an important first step and one that every junior higher can complete. It answers the question who.

At this point, you may also want to ask, "Where do you see yourself in the story? Which person are you most like?" In Mark 1:16-20, Jesus calls some fishermen to be his disciples. Besides Mark, the people in the story are Jesus, Simon, Andrew, James, John, Zebedee and the hired men. You could describe the personalities of the fishermen and then ask which one they think they are most like. Obviously, this question will be much easier to answer in some passages (for example, historical narratives) than in others; but with any passage, it will help kids put the Bible into a contemporary setting.

One reason that *People* is the first step is because it is usually quite easy to identify the people in the passage simply by reading the text, especially in historical narratives such as Genesis or Matthew. An old Chinese proverb says, 'Every journey begins with the first step.' Once we take that step, we're on our way.

People is also an important step because we, the readers, are people too. And as we read, we discover that because human nature hasn't changed over the centuries, neither have human struggles and problems. —Dave Veerman, *How to Apply the Bible*[2]

Plot

Next we move to Plot. This step answers the questions where and what and helps students understand what the passage is all about.

At this point you should explain about context—that the surrounding verses and chapters can help if the specific passage doesn't contain the answers.

In the Mark 1:1-4 example, the answer to "Where is this taking place?" is the Judean wilderness. And the answer to "What is happening?" is John the Baptist is telling everyone to be ready for the Lord's arrival by turning away from sin.

Notice that the answers for the People and Plot steps are very simple and straightforward. No one should be looking for deep, hidden meanings in the text. In effect, we are answering the question "What does the text say?" These steps help kids understand what was going on back then. Everyone in your group should be able to climb these first two steps.

Point

This is a more difficult step, but it is a crucial one for understanding and applying the Bible. Here you will be helping young people discover the biblical principle, the timeless truth, of the passage.

Explain that the point of a passage is simply the lesson, or moral, of the story. To discover the point, your young people need only ask and answer one or two questions: "What is God like?" or "What should people be like?" In other words, every Bible story will either tell us something about God and what He is like or something about people and what they should be like—how they should live. And sometimes the story will tell us both.

Returning to Mark 1:1-4, we could conclude that the point of the story is that God's plan is for people to turn from their sins in order to be ready to receive the Lord.

Let's look at Mark 3:1-6. Here we see the story of Jesus healing a man with a deformed hand. The people in the story are Jesus, a man with a deformed hand, the Pharisees, the congregation in the synagogue, the Herodians and Mark (the writer of the passage).

For the plot, we see that Jesus healed a deformed man in front of the congregation on the Sabbath in a synagogue (the Jewish house of worship) in the city of Capernaum.

For the point, we see that this story answers both questions. It tells us what God is like, because we see Jesus' anger at the Pharisees' indifference to human need and His compassion for the man with the deformed hand. The story also tells us that people should have pity on those in need and should try to help them.

Try to state the point of the story in one sentence.

It may take some time for your kids to do this step, but make sure they learn it well. Point answers the question "What does the passage mean?" and is the turning point of serious Bible study.

Present

Now that we've seen what the passage says and means, we come to "How do I apply it?" This involves the last two steps in the process.

Present means putting the story and its meaning in a contemporary setting, bringing it into the here and now. The easiest way to do this is to retrace the first three steps, by bringing them into the present. Ask, "Who could these people be today? Where could this take place today? (or "Where does this happen today?") What could be the result, here and now?" Tell kids to use their imaginations.

For example, if Jesus were to come to their neighborhoods looking for disciples, whom would He call, where would He go and what would He say? And how would they respond to His call?

Then ask how they see the point applying to today's circumstances and problems. To help answer this question, give them the following categories: family, friends, faith and future. Explain that the point of the passage will have an application in at least one of these four areas.

The point of Mark 1:1-4 is that God's plan is for people to turn from their sins in order to be ready to receive the Lord. For some this could have an impact on their *faith* as they recognize the need to turn from their sins. Some others might realize that this point could affect relationships with *friends,* feeling they should emulate John the Baptist and tell their friends about Christ.

The Mark 3:1-6 story could also affect faith and friends as we begin to have compassion for those in need.

Our fourth step, Present, takes the timeless truth and makes it timely. It brings the biblical principle into daily life.

God Speaks Through the Bible

Many are content with general applications of what they read and so do not get clear guidelines from God. We must endeavor to be specific in our applications. An example of a general application is "Christians must love their enemies." A more specific application of this same verse is "I must love Bob, even though he has been spreading slanderous stories about me. I am very busy today. But I will offer to take him and his child to see the doctor."

A second way God speaks to us is by giving us biblical principles. These are truths about topics such as what God is like and how he acts, or the nature of humans, the world, heaven, hell or the Christian life. Here God is like a teacher who presents important facts in a classroom. These facts may not have an immediate application to our lives, but we still need to take them and hide them in our hearts (Psalm 119:11). In this way we fill up a reservoir of truth in our hearts that can be tapped when the need arises. —Ajith Fernando, "Does God Speak Through the Bible?"[3]

Plan

Now we come to the last step, Plan. As mentioned earlier, this step answers the question "Now what?" It helps us decide what we are going to do to put into practice what we have learned in Point and Present. This is an action plan.

Unfortunately, most Bible application stops short of this step. People think they have applied Scripture if they come up with an "ought" statement for themselves (for example, "I ought to stop complaining"; "I ought to be nicer to my sister"; "I ought to read the Bible and pray daily"; etc.). But that's not enough.

It's great to discover the biblical principle and see how it relates to our family, friends, faith or future. But true application won't happen if we don't make a decision as to what we will actually *do* about it.

Let's say I am reading the Bible, and I become convicted about my relationship with Gail, my wife. As a result of my reading, I decide that I ought to be more loving and considerate of her. That answers "So what?" But "Now what?" (what will I do to actually put that "ought" into practice in my life?) still needs to be answered; and that's the crucial question.

To help kids with the Plan step, tell them to remember three words: PRAY, LOOK and DO. The action plan will relate to these three areas. PRAY means deciding what they can pray about. LOOK means deciding what they should look for. And DO means deciding the action they should take.

In the Mark 3:1-6 story, we saw that the point is that we should have compassion on those in need and should try to help them. This would affect PRAY, because we could ask God to open our eyes to see the needy people around us. It would also affect LOOK and DO. We should look for better ways to help those *specific* people we know who need help; and we should DO something *specific* to help them.

If I want to be more loving and considerate of my wife, my plan could include clearing the table after dinner tonight and taking her out to dinner this weekend. Those are specific actions—that's Plan.

A way to illustrate how this works together is to draw the following arrow.

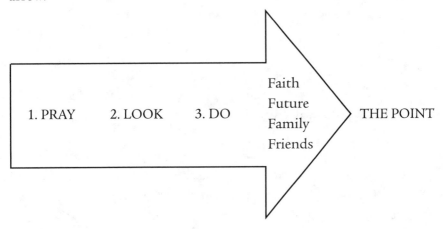

1. PRAY   2. LOOK   3. DO   Faith Future Family Friends   THE POINT

Sweet Sixteen: Strategies for Youth Education

At least 16 practical strategies are documented in Matthew 17:24-27, which tells a creative method Jesus used to pay the Temple tax and teach Peter a few lessons about Himself at the same time. These strategies represent pertinent concepts for twenty-first-century excellence in youth education.

Relational
Conversational
Confrontational
Rational
Personal
Meaningful
Controversial
Transferable

Moral
Practical
Enjoyable
Reasonable
Economical
Responsible
Mutual
Memorable

—Ronald T. Habermas, "How Should We Teach Biblical Truth"[4]

To plan means to decide what God wants us to PRAY, LOOK and DO (and then do it). That's understanding the Bible and putting it into practice in our lives.

Holding Them Accountable

As in teaching any life skill (see chapter 9), students should be given assignments and then be held accountable for doing them. This is very important for Bible application. Think of what you could have kids do, away from the meeting, to help them get into the Bible and put its principles into practice in their lives.

You could have them rewrite a chapter in their own words, read for five minutes a day, fill out a People-Plot-Point-Present-Plan sheet for a passage, memorize a verse, explain the meaning of a story to a partner or a friend, carry out the action step in Plan or complete another similar assignment.

These assignments will give them the opportunity for independent practice and will reinforce what they learned in the class.

We've found that kids do well when we've given them a little more ownership of the process. We have notebooks with our logo on the front.

We photocopy assignments and have kids keep them in the notebooks. (The notebooks are theirs to keep.) Occasionally we do special events that are "notebooks only"—only those caught up on their work may come. —Gregg Lafferty, teaching pastor, Christ Community Church, St. Charles, Illinois

When you give these assignments, however, be sure to check on how they did at the next meeting or before. You (or another staff member) could give them a call; you could assign buddies; you could have a regular check-up time in each meeting.

To make sure that kids learn to study and apply the Bible, follow up on your assignments and hold them accountable.

There are 100 million Bibles in this country, but few people read or study them. Studying the Bible is a value and a skill that most kids will not learn on their own. You can help transform lives by teaching kids how to study the Bible and apply its truths. It is God's way of making us well prepared at every point, fully equipped to do good to everyone.[5]

Think It Through

1. Why do you think it is important for kids to learn how to study the Bible?

2. When do *you* read and study the Bible? What Bible-study method do you use?

3. What does it mean to apply the Bible?

4. Who in your group would be receptive to beginning a program of personal Bible study?

5. When would be the best time and place to teach your kids how to study the Bible?

6. What could you do to help motivate your kids to study the Bible?

7. What will you do to hold kids accountable for their Bible-study assignments?

Chapter Eleven

Spitballs and Pitfalls

What has 24 arms, 24 legs and 12 heads, moves constantly and can eat you alive? The answer: 12 junior high kids. Perhaps the most terrifying prospect for any potential youth worker is facing a roomful of kids out of control. And let's face it—even one junior higher can be a monster!

- Kevin is a seventh grader with a high school body. The biggest kid in the group, he bullies everyone and insists on his own way. During Sunday School, Kevin constantly disrupts by picking on a couple of sixth graders.

- Shyness has never been a problem for Jennifer. In fact, her mouth seems to be in perpetual motion as she talks about boys, school, boys, the party last night, boys and anything else that comes up. (Did I mention boys?) And it doesn't matter where she is—youth group, concert, Sunday School, worship—Jenny and her friends talk, whisper and pass notes.
- Everyone knows what Matt will say—something gross or dirty. In every crowd breaker, discussion or conversation, he finds a way to talk about the bathroom, sex or other assorted bodily functions.
- Tanya and Paul are into cutting and throwing. Any worksheet, pencil or miscellaneous debris in their hands quickly becomes a missile to be hurled at a victim across the room.
- "Competitive" is an apt description of Carlos. Everything's a game, and he has to win. So Carlos yells, argues and even cheats to be victorious.

How many Kevins, Jennifers, Matts, Tanyas, Pauls and Carloses do you know? I'm sure you could add many of your own case studies of colorful personalities. Any one of them can disrupt a meeting and even throw it into chaos. And sometimes all of those kids will be in one youth group!

Let's face it, "junior high" and "energy" are synonymous—interruptions and disruptions are occupational hazards for anyone working with kids this age. So if you want to get through to them, you will have to know how to channel their energy and keep it under control.

Discipline Defined

Often the word "discipline" evokes pictures of drill sergeants, tough coaches, mean teachers or stern parents. Discipline is seen as punishment for stepping out of line or breaking the rules. It is negative.

But the basic meaning of "discipline" is positive. Coming from the same root as the word "disciple" (which means a learner or follower), "discipline" means organizing, training and guiding toward a goal. A runner preparing for a marathon works diligently for three months, increasing his mileage each week until he is ready for the race. He is disciplined. A concert pianist practices for hours each day to perfect her technique. She is disciplined. A salesman organizes his day and forces himself to make a certain number of calls. He is disciplined.

Discipline is important in every area of life, including youth ministry. We need to be self-disciplined, controlling ourselves and using our time and other resources well. And we should help kids become disciplined, moving them toward maturity. If you see discipline as necessary and positive action to help the ministry, you won't back away from doing what you should.

Educational

Little babies cry whenever they need anything, no matter where they are—in church, in a restaurant or in the presence of the Pope—regardless of how their screams affect others. As children grow and mature, they learn (we hope) that there are more acceptable forms of expression. Ecclesiastes 3:1 states that "there is a time for everything . . . under heaven." Kids need to know that they can't do whatever they want, whenever they want. Discipline will teach them that fact of life.

Discipline

The word "discipline" comes from the same root as "disciple." With discipline you are making disciples of your young people. Discipline often gets bad press because it's misunderstood. Discipline is not chaining young people to their seats or putting them in iron cages. People think discipline is synonymous with punishment, but in the Bible that's not the intended meaning at all. Both in the

Hebrew and the Greek the words we translate *discipline* actually mean "training" or "education." The root word "disciple" means "learner." So discipline involves instruction and training as well as correcting and it is to be motivated by love and concern.
—Les Christie, *How to Work with Rude, Obnoxious and Apathetic Kids*[1]

Freud said that maturity is the ability to postpone gratification. That's another lesson for kids to learn—sometimes they have to wait. They also need to learn that their actions lead to certain consequences. That is, they can't do anything they want and get away with it.

The teacher who insists on order instead of chaos in the classroom, the parent who makes sure that children share instead of acting selfishly, the coach who enforces the rules of the game and doesn't allow cheating and the youth leader who won't let one person spoil an activity for everyone else all give young people invaluable lessons. Discipline teaches.

Practical
Exercising crowd control just makes sense. That's why there are ushers, security guards and police officers at professional sporting events. What would a junior high meeting be like with no guidelines, rules or order? Some of the kids might have fun, but very little would be accomplished. Rules are necessary for the smooth running of the meeting or activity and for effective communication. If you want your event to meet your objective, you will need discipline.

Responsible
Working with young people is serious business. After all, each one is someone's child, a valuable creation of a loving God, and must be handled with care. Although kids may resent rules, thinking that they hinder freedom, most regulations are imposed for physical and emotional protection.

I'm sure these rules and guidelines sound familiar: no standing in front of the yellow line on the bus; no running on the pool deck; look both ways before crossing the street; don't run with scissors. Certainly those rules were created to keep children safe. Remember, as the person in charge of these young lives, you are responsible for their safety.

Fresh out of college and into youth ministry, I couldn't wait for high school camp, thinking it would be great being the counselor and buddy to the guys in the cabin. I wanted to get to know them and be their friend, so I was reluctant to be the tough guy and enforce rules such as the 11 P.M. curfew and lights out. Instead, I laughed and wrestled with them before pulling my sleeping bag over my head just after midnight. The rest of that night was a mess, as cereal, shaving cream and toilet paper flew around the room. I tried to reason with the guys in my room, but no one would listen. Finally, I left and slept elsewhere.

I know that sounds crazy, but I was afraid of alienating those guys, so I let them walk all over me. They almost destroyed the cabin in the process. Another summer, a young man almost died from a fall from an upper bunk during a pillow fight.

During those early camping experiences, I remember listening to the camp director spell out the rules at our first meeting—"no alcoholic beverages, no guys in girls' cabins or vice versa, . . ."—and I thought, *I'm glad he's doing that and not me. I don't want to be seen as the bad guy, the policeman.*

After a few dozen camps, retreats, trips and experiences like those above, however, my opinion had changed 180 degrees. I even volunteered to give the rules speech. What made the difference? I realized my responsibility as their leader and I came to see how important those rules were for everyone's safety.

As a responsible youth leader, you will need to explain and enforce certain rules.

 Responsibility requires boundaries. All human societies have boundaries, typically called laws. Without social boundaries, society would self-destruct. If everyone simply did what was right in his or her own eyes, the results would be chaotic. When the majority of people abide by the laws; that is, they are responsible citizens, the society thrives. When a significant number of individuals choose to walk their own way and live irresponsibly, the society suffers the negative consequences. . . .

. . . However, teenagers will question whether your rules are right. They will question whether your rules were made for the benefit of the teen or simply to satisfy your own whims. —Gary Chapman, *The Five Love Languages of Teenagers*[2]

Kids' Expectations

In that initial camp experience, I made the mistake common to many youth leaders—I assumed that kids are turned off by anyone exercising authority and telling them what to do. But I found the opposite to be true. They expect adults to act like adults—that includes guiding and directing them.

Some youth workers are intimidated by the kids, thinking, *Why would they listen to me and do what I say?* But remember what we covered in chapter 6—usually junior highers will respect and even obey you because of your position and because you are an adult. I'm not saying that discipline will be a piece of cake. There will be times when you may have to ask a disruptive person to leave or you may have to call his or her parents. But don't let the kids intimidate you. Even a large crowd of junior highers can be controlled by a person who speaks firmly and authoritatively and then backs up his or her words with actions.

Kids, especially junior highers, need and want adult supervision. Although they will test the limits constantly, having those limits gives them a sense of security. They know that someone is in charge and that someone cares.

Kids don't want or need an endless list of rules and someone to tell them what to do every moment of their lives. But the other extreme, no limits and total freedom, is scary, and they can't handle it.

Later in this chapter we'll cover *how* to discipline, but for now, just know that being the disciplinarian will not hurt your ministry with kids. Don't be afraid to step up to the challenge and step in to do what you must—to keep order, keep on track and move kids toward maturity. They expect it.

The Proper Climate

Effective discipline takes place in a positive climate of acceptance and affirmation. If kids know that you care about them, they will be more open to your correction and guidance.

Acceptance

Accepting someone for who he or she is does not mean that you approve of everything that person does. But your acceptance of that person will build his or her self-esteem and your relationship with him or her. Consider how God relates to us. Throughout Scripture we see evidence of God's love and acceptance, even though we ignore and disobey Him. We don't have to dress up for God or become like someone else, but we do have to repent, turning from our sin and turning to Christ. God hates the sin but loves the sinner.

Accept kids as they really are, with all their imperfections, not expecting them to be beautiful, talented and intelligent. Then help them see the error of their ways and guide them in the right direction.

Affirmation

Look for ways to affirm kids, complimenting them on what they do that is right. Discipline involves guiding and teaching. If they already are headed the right way, encourage them to keep going.

Maturity

Remember, you are an adult, so act like one. If kids break the rules, act up or even deny your authority, don't take it personally. Even if their attacks are meant to be personal, don't let them throw you off course. The quickest way to lose kids is to lose your cool. You can get them to do almost anything, but if you yell at them, call them names or use sarcasm, they will turn you off. It's not that you should never be angry with an individual or group—just be careful how you express your anger. Cutting a person down to size with a caustic remark or snide comment will only hurt your ministry with that person and with everyone watching and listening.

Humor

Although your ministry goals are serious, don't take them—or yourself—too seriously. In other words, lighten up and laugh with the kids. There is a time for enforcing rules, but there is also a time for joking and kidding around. Don't *always* be somber and serious. Let your kids see the fun side of your personality. Notice that I recommended laughing *with* kids, not at them. There's a world of difference.

 Seek a humor that relieves and uplifts young people, that glorifies Jesus Christ and brings us all together. To love young people is to want to see them laugh. But we never want a laugh at the expense of any individual or group. As we all seek to grow in this regard, may our serving be fun and our communication be sprinkled with laughs. —Dean Borgman, *When Kumbaya Is Not Enough: A Practical Theology for Youth Ministry*[3]

Acceptance, affirmation, maturity and humor will provide a positive climate for effective discipline.

How to Discipline

Establish Boundaries

Before wading into a discipline situation, think about what boundaries you want to set—what *is not* permissible behavior? Then consider what you will allow—what *is* permissible behavior? You must answer these questions completely for yourself. Then you and your staff should agree about what is and what is not acceptable.

As you discuss the expectations and rules together, keep in mind the age and development of the kids. Some movement and noise are inevitable with junior highers. At times you will have to let them act their age.

Consider your objectives, the kids and your tolerance level when you establish your boundaries.

Follow-Through

Do what you say you are going to do. This is where volunteer staff often really fall short. Junior highers can make you feel like dirt. You will think they hate you and they are no longer your friends. IMPORTANT NOTE! Junior highers bounce back unbelievably quick. Your staff needs to establish the fact that they are more than just big brothers or sisters—they are also authority figures in their lives. If this does not happen, your staff will be very frustrated, especially on overnight events. —Wayne Stuart, *Campus Life/JV Newsletter*[4]

Be Flexible

Your *real* boundaries will surface when you are with your young people. Effective crowd control and discipline are essential to the success of any junior high program, but they are not ends in themselves. During the year you may see that some rules have to be altered and some boundaries moved, either because they weren't realistic or effective or because they were counterproductive. Hard-line discipline should be used when the trusting relationship is violated, but we want kids to learn how to handle responsibilities and how to control themselves.

Your rules aren't written in stone, so be flexible and willing to change if you should.

Although discipline of young people will involve all aspects of your ministry, from this point on we will focus on meetings and events. Many of these principles can be transferred to situations with individuals.

Stage One—Before the Meeting

As you plan any event, it is important to think it through, trying to spot behavioral problems before they happen. The mix of personalities may be volatile; the setting may contribute to noise and disruptions; or the activity itself may self-destruct because of its design or contents.

Possible Troublemakers

Will those who have a history of causing trouble be there? (For example, Kevin the bully, Jennifer the talker and potty-mouth Matt.) Or will there be a troublesome combination of kids? (For example, Bryan and Kenny got into a fight last week at school; Betsy isn't speaking to Carol; and Tricia always seems to get on Andrea's nerves.) If so, how will you handle them? Of course, you can't always know the current interpersonal conflicts or who will show up. But when you do know, be prepared.

Speak to each person individually, greeting them by name. This way you are telling them, "I know you're here today. You don't have to prove it during the meeting."

Sometimes just the predominance of a certain group of kids can cause problems. In one of my high school Campus Life clubs, a large number of seniors would regularly attend. But the real leadership in the group was in the junior class, where there were many Christian kids and student leaders. The two groups seemed to get along, so there shouldn't have been many problems. But I soon found my juniors acting up and disrupting the meetings. I was confused until I realized that subconsciously the juniors had to prove that they were the insiders and the real leaders of the group. I was able to curb the problem by talking with some of them privately and enlisting their help in keeping the meetings on track.

Before you start the meeting, you may want to move some individuals to better locations. Some can't help themselves when they are by certain kids.

The Meeting Place

Are there any physical aspects of the room that may contribute to crowd-control problems? Some of these you will be able to change, and others you will have to learn to live with. Either way, thinking about them ahead of time will help you prepare for the worst.

For example, a room with a tile or cement floor tends to be quite noisy. That's because the acoustics are poor and the kids are uncomfortable if they have to sit on the floor. If they sit in chairs on the cement, the sound of the chairs scraping on the floor can be maddening. This particular problem can be corrected by changing rooms, bringing carpet squares or pillows to sit on or giving kids a chance to move around more during the meeting.

Lighting can also be a help or a hindrance. The front of the room, where the leader stands or sits, should be well lit. This will help keep everyone's attention focused. If the leader speaks from the shadows, kids will find it easier to stop listening.

If you have a youth room at church, you can design it for minimal problems and maximum effectiveness. If you meet in homes, however, you should visit the home before the meeting, so you'll know what to expect. Then get there about a half hour beforehand to make any necessary changes.

Follow these guidelines when considering the location. Most host parents will gladly cooperate if you let them know far enough in advance what your needs are.

- Do not allow pets and younger children in the meeting. Nothing will divert kids' attention like a cute baby or puppy that has wandered into the room.
- Make sure the radio and television cannot be heard in your meeting room. In fact, don't even have it turned on in the room beforehand. Kids will get into a show and want to leave it on; and if they can hear a show or a favorite song in another room, they will talk about it—immediately.
- Do not allow the preparation of the refreshments to be a distraction. Sometimes parents will have candy and other snack foods in bowls around the room. That's a mistake. Kids will spend more time passing the bowls and eating (and throwing the M&Ms) than listening. And nothing is more distracting than hearing soft drinks being poured in the next room or hearing and smelling popcorn as it is being popped in the kitchen.
- Choose a room that is conducive for what you have planned (and vice versa). In other words, if your crowd breakers need space and involve a lot of moving around, don't try to do them in a small room. Choose a room that is big enough for your crowd. Junior highers don't appreciate being wedged together, especially when they have to sit next to certain kids. You don't want a huge room for a tiny group, but you do want them to feel comfortable. In the meeting, don't allow anyone to lie down.
- If possible, push sofas to the wall and remove the rest of the furniture from the room, especially the breakables. You probably will need the space, and remember, kids will sit on anything (even coffee tables).
- Choose a front for the meeting that is opposite the entrance and the refreshment area, with a wall behind you (not a window). This is where you will run the

meeting. You should be able to see everyone from that spot. In other words, don't allow kids to sit behind you; behind chairs, couches and so forth; or in stairways or alcoves. In fact, don't let kids sit behind anything or anybody or turn their backs to you. If they can't see you, they think you can't see them.

- Think about other possible distractions. As you check out the room, look for anything that can cause a problem (for example, children's toys, firewood, stack of magazines, CDs, tapes, souvenirs, etc.).

When our church met in a local high school, the Sunday School used classrooms—complete with teachers' desks piled high with test papers, stacks of textbooks, maps and posters on the walls and other miscellaneous trappings of school. Besides all the obvious potential distractions, we found that our junior high kids didn't appreciate meeting in that setting, because Sunday School reminded them too much of school. At first we tried to remedy the situation by pulling the chairs in a circle. We also tried having everyone sit on the floor. But the solution that worked the best was to move the class to a hallway. Everyone would bring a chair (the floor was carpeted), and I provided clipboards and pencils for any writing that had to be done. The class was much more attentive and cooperative.

In that particular situation, the classroom itself was a distraction.

Attention Span

Because the attention span of junior highers is short, analyze the program to make sure it will hold their attention. If you spot possible lulls in the action, change the program or decide how you will keep everyone interested during the slower times.

A few years ago, I sat as an observer in the back of a junior high Sunday School class. There were only eight kids, a teacher and an adult helper. The lesson for that Sunday centered on worksheets that the teacher distributed. Here's how the class responded:

- Three kids made paper airplanes with the worksheets.
- One girl poked holes in her paper, in a circular pattern, until the paper fell apart.
- A sixth-grade girl put the worksheet on her desk, put her head down on her arm on top of the paper and closed her eyes.
- An eighth-grade boy rolled up the paper to form a telescope and looked at the teacher through it—then he stuck his pencil through the paper and twirled it in a circle.
- A seventh grader flipped the paper up into the air until it fell on the floor—then he repeated the process over and over.
- An eighth-grade girl was too busy drawing a picture on another sheet of paper to notice the worksheet on her desk.

Crowd Breakers

Certain games and activities lend themselves to rowdiness. Because we want kids to have a good time at our meetings, many of our crowd breakers will be of that variety. If we know what to expect, however, we will know how to head off any problems.

If you are having an eating contest, what will you do with the peels, leftover food or used marshmallows? Is the game sloppy? How will kids clean up? Does the race get everyone hot, sweaty and wound up? How will you cool them off and calm them down?

A couple of guys came to our Campus Life office and asked if they could run a version of Campus Life for the junior high school in their neighborhood. We gave them our blessing and a few suggestions (but not a lot of guidance). Their first activity was a pillow fight in the school gym. Hundreds of kids showed up, and before too long, feathers were everywhere. For months afterward, feathers were blown out of the heating ducts. Needless to say, the school never forgot it. We and our well-motivated, enthusiastic college volunteers had not thought through the crowd-control implications of the activity.

If you are using props, be sure to have your props handy, so you won't have to take time to get them together. And after a game, have a staff person pick up anything that can be broken, torn, flipped, popped or thrown.

Discussion and Wrap-Up

I covered this in chapter 8, so I won't repeat myself, but this is where most discipline problems occur. It's not easy to get the group to calm down and get serious, and every noise and movement seems to be magnified.

It may be that you're trying to have a discussion, and someone acts up; you pass out worksheets, but Tanya and Paul tear them up before they are all distributed; you want to give a short wrap-up, but no one is paying attention. What can you do to head off these problems before they occur?

This is where staff placement is especially important. They can assist kids with their work and help keep order. Make sure that they are prepared to get in place at this time in the meeting.

Refreshments

With this age group, it's not a good idea just to dismiss everyone and send them to refreshments. Usually that will cause a stampede. At one of our youth group meetings, the boys got to the food first and ate all the donuts.

Instead, think of an orderly way for everyone to be served. You could have them go by teams (winning team first), or you could have staff members posted at key locations. Tell everyone how and where to get in line and explain that they should take only one (drink, piece of pizza, sandwich, cup of popcorn and so forth) until everyone has been served.

By thinking ahead and anticipating potential trouble spots before the meeting, you will be able to prevent most discipline problems.

Stage Two—During the Meeting

Clear Ground Rules

As we have discussed earlier, junior highers are used to being told what to do and usually will respect authority. They expect you to have rules and guidelines. But they need to be told beforehand what those rules are. Explain clearly and seriously what you expect and the consequences of misbehaving. Kids should know the limits and that they will be enforced.

At camp, the main rules should be outlined during the first large group meeting. In a Sunday School class you may want to repeat the general rules at certain points during the year (at least once every quarter). One Sunday School teacher led a discussion of the rules that the class felt they should have for their time together. After they agreed on the list, he wrote the rules on a piece of poster board that he hung on the wall.

At these times, the enforcement procedures and consequences should also be explained. Put this in writing and give copies to the parents.

Special guidelines also should be explained during most of the meetings, either because of a unique activity or because kids need to be reminded. For example, in the high school Campus Life meetings, before every discussion, I would say something like, "As you know, during these discussions we have a few simple rules. First, you raise your hand and then speak when I call on you; second, only one person speaks at a time; and third, you may use no offensive language or put-downs."

When you explain the rules, ask for everyone's cooperation and obedience; don't demand it. Be positive and explicit, and remember that relationships will help in crowd control and discipline. The best crowd control is done by the students themselves. Work at building the loyalties of a core group of kids who will stand behind you.

Behavior Management

Unwanted behavior can be avoided through proper understanding of what causes it. The following list contains questions to ask about your own behavior and how it might help you control undesirable behavior in your kids.

1. Do I know my students individually?
2. What have I done recently to help build the self-esteem of the kids?
3. Are my students involved in the meeting? Have I given them responsibility? Have they had a part in the formation of guidelines? Planning? Activities?
4. Have I shown love and acceptance toward each person?
5. What expressions of praise and encouragement have I used?
6. Am I aware of my kids' interests as I plan activities?
7. What different media have I used in the past? Which could I use in the future?
8. What might be the reason for past unwanted behavior?
9. How do I allow for individual creativity?
10. In what ways do I stimulate "right brain" students?
11. Could I stand to change something about my appearance?
12. What is the most effective use of the room arrangement?
13. What do I have ready for the first arrival each week?

—Nancy McGuirk, "Managing Unwanted Classroom Behavior"[5]

Fast Action

When you are confronted with a problem, respond immediately. Don't ignore it or hope it will disappear.

With an individual, be firm and confrontive but not pushy. Keep your cool and don't ridicule or talk down to the offender. Also, warn the person only once. Then if he or she misbehaves again, take action. Here are some possible ways to respond to minor infractions (excessive whispering, poking a friend, tearing paper, untying someone's shoes and so forth):

- Address the person by name and say, "That is not acceptable. The next time it happens, I will have to _____."
- Have a staff member sit next to the misbehaving individual.
- Have a staff member put a hand on that person's shoulder and ask him or her to settle down.
- Move the offender to another part of the room or next to you.

If the individual continues to misbehave or the problem is more serious (for example, talking back, cheating, swearing, pushing, hitting, being verbally abusive, etc.), have one of the staff members take the offender out of the room to talk things over.

During that talk, the staff person should ask if the individual knows why he or she had to leave the room. If the individual will not admit that what he or she did was wrong, the staff person should say, "Here's what I saw you do . . ."

Next, the staff person should ask, "Is what you were doing disruptive to, or distracting from, what the group is doing?" If the young person says no or tries to minimize the behavior, the staff person should explain that, in his or her opinion, it *is* disruptive.

Next, the staff person should ask, "Is what you were doing against our rules?" and "Can we allow you to continue doing that?" If the person doesn't see that what he or she did was wrong, the staff person should explain that what he or she did *is* against the rules and cannot be allowed to continue.

Finally, the staff person should ask, "Are you willing to work it out?" If the young person is cooperative, then the two of them should come to an understanding about what can be done to improve the situation and what will happen if it doesn't improve.

If this doesn't prove to be effective with a young person and he or she continues to disobey and disrupt, you should bring his or her parents into the situation.

Whatever you do, *don't* use physical punishment (spanking, hitting, shoving, etc.). This will hurt your ministry in more ways than I can cover here. A touch or a firm grip will say that you mean business.

With the group, the best way to respond to a problem is to use the goodwill of the whole group as positive peer pressure. Remind them of the ground rules and explain that you want to treat them as adults. During the discussion or wrap-up, you can pause or stop and look at the floor, waiting for everyone to quiet down. Speaking louder or saying "Quiet!" usually won't work. It will also be helpful to move staff to trouble spots.

Incentives work well with junior highers and can help in crowd control. That's why Campus Life/JV meetings end with The Biggie, an exciting crowd breaker. Kids know that they will get to The Biggie if they have time. And there will only be enough time if the leader doesn't have to keep getting everyone quiet and organized.

Outside of the meeting, you could spend some relationship-building time with certain kids who tend to cause problems, talking to them about their behavior.

If the group continues to be disruptive, you may have to end the meeting early, eliminating the last activity or refreshments. This should only be done as a last resort.

Our JV club seemed to be getting out of control. Every week we spent more time dealing with noise and discipline problems. The kids weren't antagonistic—they just couldn't control themselves. Because the meetings were supposed to be 45 minutes long (then we had refreshments and the parents came to pick them up), we explained that we would have to move things along, and we tried to enlist their cooperation. But one night, I had had enough. Right in the middle of another staff person's talk, I announced that the meeting was over and that they all had to get their coats and leave. (I used a firm and serious tone of voice; I didn't sound angry.) There was no time for refreshments—some of the parents were already outside. The kids were stunned by the abruptness of my announcement, and they left in serious silence. The subsequent meetings were much easier to control.

Positive Reinforcement

Discipline should not be limited to correcting negative actions. When kids do what is right, praise them. In fact, look for ways to compliment young people, publicly and privately. You can show approval for what they are doing by saying something, patting them on the back or just giving them a knowing nod or wink. And you could use a special activity as a reward for a young person who makes progress.

Reinforcement/Affirmation

Kids who get an abundance of praise and affirmation for positive behavior will be more likely to repeat it. Affirmation truly is a powerful motivator that not only encourages positive behavior but also builds self-esteem. —Wayne Rice, *Cleared for Takeoff* [6]

This is very important with those who have caused problems in the past and are showing improvement. After a meeting you could say something like:

- "Meredith, I really appreciated the way you participated in the discussion. You had a lot of good things to say."

- "Josh, I see real progress in the way you've been acting in youth group. Thanks for trying."
- "Thanks, Ernestine, for helping quiet everyone down. The younger kids look up to you—you're a leader."

You could also reward the entire group for being attentive, following through on an assignment or doing what is right in a certain situation. Hand out candy, take them to McDonald's, hold a party or reward them in some other way. These group rewards can also be effective as incentives (for example, "if we _____, then we'll have a party").

Stage Three—After the Meeting

After every meeting or event, you should have a time of evaluation with your staff. This doesn't have to take a lot of time, but make it a habit. Discuss what went well, what needs improvement and what you should do next time.

For discipline purposes this process is especially important. Talk through the problems, determining their causes and deciding on future actions.

Afterward it is also important to follow through with the individuals who caused the problems. Talking things over with them can be very helpful and can build the relationships. In certain cases, you may want to inform the parents about what you are seeing and enlist their support. You want Mom and Dad on your team. You *don't* want them forming wrong conclusions about you and the group because of a casual or even hateful remark by their son or daughter.

- "Mr. Franklin, Dennis may have told you that I had to send him out of the room tonight at youth group. I wanted to let you know what happened and why I did what I did."

- "Mrs. Rose, I really like Stephanie, and I'm glad she's involved in the group. But, quite frankly, recently she's been disrupting the meetings with some of her comments. I was wondering if we could spend a little time talking about the situation and how we can work together to help her."
- "Mrs. Green, I think that you, your husband, Tony and I should sit down soon and talk about Tony's behavior at church. You and I have talked before, but I think we should all get together, clear the air and see what we can do to help Tony control his actions."

Evaluation and follow-through after the meeting will help prevent future discipline problems.

Discipline is vital for having an effective ministry with junior highers. Without limits, boundaries, rules, guidelines and consequences, they will run wild. That's the way they are—young and full of energy.

When a Group Member Destroys Property

Require young people to repair, clean up or pay for the damage they have done—and more. For instance, if a young person writes on a wall, he should be required to wash all the walls in the room. If a student stuck gum under her chair, she should be required to scrape off all the gum in the room. If a kid breaks a window, he should pay for it. The young person will have to work out a way to pay back damages. This can be paid in cash or the expense for repairs could be worked off— perhaps earning $5.00 an hour by doing work around the church. —Les Christie, *How to Work with Rude, Obnoxious and Apathetic Kids*[7]

Discipline is also a part of ministry itself. As positive action, it teaches young people self-control and guides them toward maturity.

Don't be afraid to exercise your authority, define your boundaries and enforce the rules. Kids need it and expect it.

Think It Through

1. Who or what helped you become self-disciplined?

2. What is there about your regular (or typical) meeting place that contributes to crowd-control problems? What can you do to correct or minimize those features?

3. Who in your group usually causes discipline problems in your meetings? Why do you think each of these individuals acts that way?

4. How might your ministry team work together to minimize crowd-control problems?

5. What would you do if a young person became a persistent trouble-maker?

6. What signs do you see that some of your kids are maturing and starting to become self-disciplined?

Chapter Twelve

Invisible Kids

"Doctor, doctor!" shouted the nurse, her voice filled with breathless excitement. "There's an invisible man in the waiting room!" Calmly the doctor replied, "Tell him I can't see him." We may chuckle at a corny joke like that because we know that invisible people don't exist. Or do they?

"Invisible" simply means something that is not seen. And often we can be blind to things all around us. They are there, but they are out of sight. Thus, for all practical purposes, those things are invisible. Some time ago, I had heard that minivans were selling well, but I hadn't really noticed. When I was thinking about buying one, however, I saw them everywhere. When I was hospitalized for a kidney stone, I thought my condition was rare. But soon it seemed as though everybody I met had suffered through one of these excruciating attacks.

Minivans and kidney stones were around me, but I hadn't noticed. Then, sensitized by personal involvement, my eyes were opened. Lack of personal involvement can limit our perspective.

Things and people can also be invisible to us because we're too busy to see. Preoccupied with schedules and goals, we rush through our hectic lives with tunnel vision. Everything on the periphery blurs.

I remember wondering how I could have been so blind to a certain friend's need. Looking back, it was obvious that his body language, his actions and even his words were shouting "Help!" But I didn't see or hear the signs. My thoughts and concentration were elsewhere and not on him. Life's busyness can block our vision.

Invisibility can also come from an act of the will—a conscious choice to look the other way.

A line in Bob Dylan's classic song "Blowin' in the Wind" asks us "how many times can a man turn his head, pretending he just doesn't see?" I don't know how many times that happens, but I do know that it happens often. Faced with needy people in a hurting world, men and women turn away and act as though nothing is wrong. They pretend that the problem doesn't exist, or they hope that it will go away. Choice also determines what we see.

I bring up invisibility because I am concerned about the invisible kids—young men and women who are passed over, neglected and avoided—early adolescents.

Early in this book, I explained how adults heap attention on little children, watching with wonder the miracle of growth and praising their progress. But junior highers aren't cute anymore. In fact, many of them are downright homely, awkward and obnoxious, as they grow in fits and starts through those wonder years. And they certainly don't act cute! They need affirmation more than ever, but they have become invisible to the adults around them.

At the other end of the continuum, churches usually hire professionals to work with the high schoolers. With a wonderful array of exciting programs, activities, events and trips, a fully orbed ministry hums through the year like a well-oiled machine. So even the church budget might ignore early adolescents, leapfrogging over the invisible kids and lavishing attention on older teens.

But at this time in their young lives, they need the love and concern— the ministry—of caring adults. Growing rapidly in all areas, they need support and acceptance. Learning to think and evaluate, they need answers. Making critical choices, they need guidance. Facing pressures and temptations, they need strength and encouragement. And in all of this, they need Christ.

This book has been written to open your eyes to these invisible young people—to motivate and mobilize you to reach out to kids before they move into high school.

We have looked at the need for the ministry and the characteristics of early adolescents. We have discussed the planning process, the role of parents and building the ministry team. We have considered how to build relationships, share the gospel and run meetings. And we have learned how to teach life skills and the Bible and how to discipline.

In addition, in each chapter I have included a Think It Through section, questions for personal analysis and ministry strategy. I hope you have taken time to answer the questions thoughtfully and honestly.

But now the reading and writing are finished; it's time to move out and move into their world. It's time for action—to reach kids and to share the vision with others.

For whatever reason, don't turn off or turn away from this generation. They shouldn't be invisible kids anymore.

Resources

For Youth Workers

Ministry Training Opportunities

All of these seminars carry a healthy price tag, but they're worth it. When you call or write, be sure to ask about the junior high ministry courses.

Dynamic Communicators Workshop; Ken Davis/DCW, 6080 W. 82nd Drive, Arvada, CO 80003; (303) 425-1319; www.kendavis.com

Taught by Mr. Dynamic Communicator himself (and others), these workshops train adults in the fine art of speaking, especially to youth. They are held at a variety of locations and are listed at the website under "Training."

Group Publishing; 1515 Cascade Ave.; Loveland, CO 80538; (970) 669-3836 or (800) 447-1070; www.grouppublishing.com

Group offers many fine training opportunities. Every year, Group-sponsored trainers and speakers travel to hundreds of cities to provide powerful training for children's workers, youth workers, educators and pastors. Group schedules workshop tours and offers custom training through its speakers bureau.

Sonlife Ministries; 526 N. Main; Elburn, IL 60119; (800) 770-4769 or (630) 365-5855 in Illinois; www.sonlife.com

Sonlife is dedicated to "helping the local church reach and disciple for Jesus Christ." Their seminars include Growing a Healthy Church; Growing a Healthy Youth Ministry; Youth Equipping Events Global; Youth Initiative; and Youth Ministry Feedback. Seminar schedules are available at their website.

YouthBuilders; 32236 Paseo Adelanto, Suite D; San Juan Capistrano, CA 92675; (949) 487-0217; www.youthbuilders.com (formerly known as National Institute of Youth Ministry, or NIYM)

The goal of this organization, led by ministry veteran Jim Burns, is to train, equip and assist youth workers to have a more effective ministry with youth and their families. Programs include two-week training courses (with a maximum of 24 people in each course) and a series of two-day Intensives across the country.

Youth for Christ/USA; P.O. Box 228822; Denver, CO 80222; (303) 843-9000—www.gospelcom.net/yfc

Every summer, Youth for Christ (YFC) trains its new staff and other youth workers at their Summer Institute of Youth Evangelism. The schedule includes a junior high track for those specializing in that ministry. YFC also has Campus Life/JV training videos available. Specific training events are listed at their website under "Events" for teens and staff.

Youth Specialties; 300 S. Pierce, El Cajon, CA 92921; (619) 440-2333; www.youthspecialties.com

Besides publishing many fine resources, this youth ministry organization sponsors National Youth Workers Conventions and one-day National Resource seminars all across America.

Books

Barna, George. *Third Millennium Teens: Research on the Minds, Hearts, and Souls of America's Teenagers.* **Ventura, CA: The Barna Research Group, Ltd., 1999 (soon to be published by Gospel Light/Regal Books, Ventura, CA).**

The subtitle adequately describes the work. Those who work with young teens will glean valuable information from this study.

Borgman, Dean. *When Kumbaya Is Not Enough, A Practical Theology for Youth Ministry.* **Peabody, MA: Hendrickson Publishing, 1997.**

An ideal youth-ministry text, this book is accessible and helpful for all youth workers. Dean Borgman has taught at Gordon-Conwell Theological Seminary for many years and has worked with Young Life. He also founded the Center for Youth Studies. Dean is an internationally recognized authority on youth culture and adolescent ministries.

Burns, Jim. *The Youth Builder.* **Eugene, OR: Harvest House Publishers, 1988 (to be revised and re-released in 2001 by Gospel Light/Regal Books).**

In this book, Jim has drawn on his experience as a veteran youth minister and has given us an excellent resource for planning, organizing and implementing a church youth ministry. It is comprehensive, covering everything from understanding relational youth ministry to building relationships and planning programs.

Christie, Les. *How to Work with Rude, Obnoxious and Apathetic Kids.* **Wheaton, IL: Victor Books, 1988.**

As discussed in chapter 11, discipline is a critical area in working with early adolescents. This book gives a wealth of practical help for dealing with young people of all ages, including how to be a positive disciplinarian, how to deal with anger, how to get rid of distractions and how to deal with specialized problems.

Crabtree, Jack. *Better Safe than Sued.* **Loveland, CO: Group Publishing, Inc., 1998.**

Jack dispenses timely and sensible advice for the youth leader who wants to avoid mishaps caused by haphazard planning and poor judgment. He covers a wide range of subjects: insurance coverage, screening and training staff, vehicle safety, camping, and water sports. This is a must read for any youth worker—professional or volunteer.

Dausey, Gary, ed. *The Youth Leader's Source Book*. Grand Rapids, MI: Zondervan Publishing House, 1991.

Drawing on the wisdom of a number of youth experts, Gary provides us with a complete view of youth ministry. More than presenting a philosophy, this book gives practical ideas for building a foundation, developing an environment, planning activities and sharpening skills.

Davis, Ken. *How to Speak to Youth . . . And Keep Them Awake at the Same Time*. Grand Rapids, MI: Zondervan Publishing, 1996.

One of the best speakers in America, Ken offers guidelines and a step-by-step approach for preparing and delivering talks to young people. The book is also available on Ken's website: www.kendavis.com.

Dunn, Richard R. and Mark H. Senter III, eds. *Reaching a Generation for Christ*. Chicago: Moody Press, 1997.

Written to replace *The Complete Book of Youth Ministry*, this impressive work provides a framework for youth ministry, two types of youth ministry structures, the context for adult leaders in youth ministry, skills necessary for changing existing youth ministries, five challenges faced by youth ministers, and resources for youth ministry.

Hicks, Dr. Rick and Kathy. *Boomers, Xers, and Other Strangers: Understanding the Generational Differences that Divide Us*. Wheaton, IL: Tyndale House Publishers, 1999.

Explains the different attributes of the various levels of the present youth culture.

Hine, Thomas. *The Rise and Fall of the American Teenager*. New York: Avon Books, Inc., 1999.

Another book that explores the youth culture.

Hymowitz, Kay S. *Ready or Not, Why Treating Children as Small Adults Endangers Their Future and Ours.* New York: The Free Press, 1999.
Addresses the misconception that children are merely small adults and explains why that is dangerous premise.

Mueller, Walt. *Understanding Today's Youth Culture.* Wheaton, IL: Tyndale House Publishers, 1999.
Written by the founder and president of the Center for Parent/Youth Understanding, this impressive work is helpful for parents and youth workers. As the title promises, it examines today's youth culture and gives practical suggestions for ministering to teens who are immersed in that culture.

Neff, Miriam. *Helping Teens in Crisis.* Wheaton, IL: Tyndale House Publishers, 1993.
This book is written for Christian adults who care about troubled young people and want to reach them for Christ.

Olson, Keith. *Counseling Teenagers.* Loveland, CO: Group Books, 1984.
This is an exhaustive reference work for counseling, covering a multitude of problems and situations.

Rice, Wayne. *Junior High Ministry: A Guide to Early Adolescence for Youth Workers.* Grand Rapids, MI: Zondervan Publishing House, 1998.
This updated and expanded edition of this book takes a comprehensive look at early adolescence and how to minister to kids during those tumultuous years. Wayne is known as Mr. Junior High Ministry, and he has done an excellent job of combining the theoretical with the practical.

Smith, Tim. *Seven Cries of Today's Teens: Inside the Millennial Generation*. Wheaton, IL: Tyndale House Publishers, 2001.

Bolstered by research from George Gallup, Jr., this book provides a holistic look at teenagers in the twenty-first century, dealing with their social, cultural, emotional and spiritual lives. It offers practical help for parents, mentors and youth workers.

Strommen, Merton P. and A. Irene. *Five Cries of Parents*. San Francisco, CA: Harper and Row, 1985.

Written as a result of an extensive study of early adolescents and their parents by the Search Institute, this book provides a wealth of in-depth information for both youth workers and parents. Each chapter analyzes the data, draws conclusions about the needs of youth and parents and gives practical advice for building a more satisfying life together.

Veerman, David. *How to Apply the Bible*. Grand Rapids, MI: Baker Books, 1999.

With the goal of helping readers discover the truths of Scripture and put them into practice, this book presents two Bible study methods, the Pyramid and the Window. The practical principles in this book will benefit both adults and teenagers.

Magazines

Group (Loveland, CO: Group Publishing)

Published bimonthly, this magazine is geared directly to youth ministry. Each issue contains helpful articles on youth ministry, ideas and meeting plans.

YouthWorker journal (El Cajon, CA: Youth Specialties)

Although written for professional youth workers, most of whom work with senior highers, each issue of this quarterly journal contains much that applies to junior high ministry. "Focus on Junior High" is a regular column.

Internet

Helpful websites include:
> www.tbcl.com (The Best Christian Links)
> www.botcw.com (The Best of the Christian Web)
> www.christianity.com
> www.gospelcom.net (Gospel Communications Network)
> www.gospelcom.net/ifc (Internet for Christians)
> www.pulseyouth.com
> www.youthpastor.com

Sunday School Curricula

Each of the evangelical Christian curricula publishing companies has a line of curriculum for junior highers or young teens. The lessons are helpful because they are Bible oriented, they give the teacher guidance, they provide a number of resources, and they usually include teaching suggestions and information about young people. The problem with most of the lessons, however, is that they tend to use a lot of paper (worksheets for the students to use in class), try to cover too much and/or are often very conceptual. So I recommend that teachers use the curriculum as a guide and a resource but not follow it verbatim. Whatever material you choose will be most effective if it is adapted to your class and edited to meet the needs of junior high kids.

David C. Cook; 4050 Lee Vance View, Colorado Springs, CO 80918; (800) 708-5550, www.cookministries.com

Gospel Light; 2300 Knoll Drive, Ventura, CA 93003; (800) 446-7735, www.gospellight.com

Group Publishing; 1515 Cascade, Loveland, CO 80538; (800) 447-1070, www.grouppublishing.com

Standard Publishing; 8121 Hamilton Avenue, Cincinnati, OH 45231; (800) 482-2060, www.standardpub.com

There are also many fine denominational publishers. All of these companies will be happy to send you a catalog and a sample of their material upon request.

Meeting Planning Aids

LessonMaker Youth Meetings. **Austin, TX: iExalt, Inc., 2000.**
This CD-Rom is loaded with all the meetings from the *Any Old Time*, *Flex Sessions* and *Serious Fun* books and hundreds of other activities, organized by topics. For more information, call (800) 888-9898 or visit www.WORDsearchBible.com.

Gospel Light
The latest in junior high curricula, *Pulse* is dedicated to presenting God's Word for a junior high world. Each book contains six lessons on an important topic in one of three major areas—biblical studies (e.g., *Teens of the Bible* and *Miracles of Jesus*), life issues studies (e.g., *Life at School* and *Friends*) and discipleship studies (e.g., *The Great Commission* and *Fruit*

of the Spirit). Each study also contains youth-leader tips and articles, options, active learning and evangelism activities for every session.

Group Publishing

This publisher offers several books of games, activities and ideas including *High-Energy Meetings for Young Teenagers, Easy to Use and Fun to Do Jr. High Meetings, Quick Crowdbreakers, Games for Youth Groups* and Group's *Best Jr. High Meetings*. Be sure to choose only those activities that will work well with your kids. Group also publishes Active Bible Curriculum and Core Belief Bible Study Series for this age.

Youth Specialties

Youth Specialties (YS) has an Ideas Library and several other books of games, crowd breakers, skits, etc. Again, most of these are geared for high school, so carefully select the ones you will use.

For Parents

Most of the following books can be found in Christian bookstores. The magazines, however, should be ordered directly from the publishers.

Books

Baehr, Ted. *The Media-Wise Family*. Colorado Springs, CO: Chariot Victor Publishing, 1998.

An award-winning producer, writer and director, Dr. Baehr is the head of the Christian Film and Television Commission. Billed as the "Christian family guide to making morally and spiritually responsible decisions about movies, TV and multimedia," this book is an invaluable resource for helping parents and teenagers evaluate the media and its effects on their lives. The commission also produces *Movie Guide* newsletter and a variety of audiocassettes and videocassettes. For more information, go to www.movieguide.org.

Chapman, Gary. *The Five Love Languages of Teenagers*. Chicago: Northfield Publishing, 2000.

Written by the author of the best-selling *The Five Love Languages*, this book promises to help parents "discover powerful ways to nurture your teen's inner spirit and learn how you can fill his or her love tank to overflowing."

Faber, Adele, and Elaine Mazlish. *How to Talk So Kids Will Listen and Listen So Kids Will Talk*. New York: Avon Books, 1982.

Although this isn't a Christian book and the age range is broader than junior high, it contains much information that parents can use in communicating with and disciplining their children.

McIntire, Roger. *Losing Control of Your Teenager: Ten Rules for Raising an Adult While Keeping a Friend*. Amherst, MA: HRD Press, 1985.

The subtitle tells it all. This book is about helping kids develop and mature—loving them while letting them go. Again, this is not a Christian book, but any parent should find it quite helpful.

Olson, Keith. *What Makes Your Teenager Tick?* Loveland, CO: Group Books, 1988.

Although this book focuses on teenagers (while most junior highers are 11 or 12), the content will be very helpful to parents, especially those wondering how to handle a teenager in the house. Keith divides kids into eight personality types and gives insight and practical guidelines for relating to each type.

Rice, Wayne and David Veerman. *Understanding Your Teenager.* Nashville, TN: Word Publishing, 1999.

Patterned after the seminar of the same name, this book provides an in-depth look into adolescence and youth culture and offers practical steps that parents can take to relate to their teens. For information on the seminar, call (800) 561-9309 or go to www.uyt.com.

Sanders, Bill. *Seize the Moment, Not Your Teen.* Wheaton, IL: Tyndale House Publishers, 1997.

Drawing on his years of experience as one of America's most gifted youth-communicators, Bill has provided parents with an outstanding resource teaches the art of opportunity parenting.

Schimmels, Cliff. *When Junior Highs Invade Your Home.* Ada, MI: Baker Books, Fleming H. Revell Company, 1990.

Using a case-study format, Dr. Schimmels (veteran educator and author) presents a realistic picture of junior high young people and gives practical advice for reacting to this age group and relating to them. This book is inexpensive, easy to read and very helpful.

Smiley, Kendra. *Helping Your Kids Make Good Choices.* Ann Arbor, MI: Vine Books, 2000.

Well-known speaker and mother of three teenage boys, Kendra helps parents build a solid foundation with their kids for making Christ-honoring choices.

Veerman, David R. *Tough Parents for Tough Times.* Wheaton, IL: Tyndale House Publishers, 2000.

In a world where anything goes, parents often become intimidated into inaction by what their children and others might think. This book will give parents courage to hold the line with their teenagers on tough issues.

Williams, Dorothy and Lyle. *Helping Your Teenager Succeed in School.* **Loveland, CO: Group Books, 1989.**

Drawing on Dorothy's work with Search Institute, Lyle's work as a junior high school counselor and their experience as parents of three teenagers, the Williamses present friendly, practical advice to help parents help their teenagers get the most out of school.

Magazines

Focus on the Family. **Colorado Springs, CO: Focus on the Family.**

This monthly communiqué from the ministry of the same name contains helpful advice for parents and often offers resources that parents of junior highers would find helpful. To subscribe, call Focus on the Family at (800) 232-6459 or go to www.family.org. Focus on the Family also hosts Life on the Edge conferences for teens and parents to attend together throughout the United States.

Plugged In. **Colorado Springs, CO: Focus on the Family.**

The purpose of this monthly Focus on the Family publication is to help parents and youth leaders guide teens through the world of popular youth culture. To subscribe, call (800) 232-6459 or go to www.family.org/pluggedin.

Today's Father. **National Center for Fathering.**

Each issue contains insightful articles and practical help for fathers of children of all ages. For more information and to subscribe, call (913) 384-4661 or go to www.fathers.com.

Internet

familyclick.com

This is a website to help parents screen the Web.

family.org

This is the Focus on the Family ministry website with lots of information of importance to Christian families.

For Junior Highers

Books

Unfortunately, most young people don't read very much on their own, so anything written for them must grab their attention. A book that you might consider is by Ken Davis, *How to Live with Your Parents Without Losing Your Mind* (Grand Rapids, MI: Zondervan Publishing House, 1988). It is a humorous and realistic book with cartoons scattered throughout.

Dobson, James. *Preparing for Adolescence*. Ventura, CA: Regal Books, 1999.

This classic is a must read for preadolescents and their parents. Dr. Dobson discusses the topics that concern kids most. Also available are companion group or family study guides and audiocassettes.

Schmitt, Betsy. *Sticky Situations*. Wheaton, IL: Tyndale House Publishers, 1997.

This volume contains 365 interactive devotions that help kids make good choices in the hard situations in life.

Veerman, Dave and Wayne Rice. *Reality 101.* **Wheaton, IL: Tyndale House Publishers, 1999.**

The authors answer 101 questions posed by teens on God, family, friends, future, self-image, money, music, prayer, school and the world.

Washington, Linda M. and Dave Veerman. *Ready for Life.* **Wheaton, IL: Tyndale House Publishers, 1998.**

This is a fun devotional book that teaches important life skills through real-life stories.

Wilson, Neil S. and Dave Veerman. *The Student's Guide to the Bible.* **Wheaton, IL: Tyndale House Publishers, 1999.**

This is a 350-page, yet compact, Bible handbook.

Magazines

Breakaway. **Colorado Springs, CO: Focus on the Family.**

This magazine published by Focus on the Family is aimed directly at junior high boys. To order, call Focus on the Family at (800) 232-6459 or go to www.family.org.

Brio. **Colorado Springs, CO: Focus on the Family.**

Published monthy, *Brio* is the junior high girls' counterpart to *Breakaway*. To order, call Focus on the Family at (800) 232-6459 or go to www.family.org.

Campus Life. **Carol Stream, IL: Christianity Today.**

This magazine is written for older high school students, but eighth graders might be able to relate. This is an outstanding publication, filled with well-written and practical articles each month. A leader's guide is also available. Consider giving one-year subscriptions to *Campus Life* to all your graduating eighth graders. Write to Campus Life at 465 Gunderson Drive, Carol Stream, IL 60188, or call (630) 260-6181.

Guideposts for Teens. **Carmel, NY: Guideposts Publications.**

This magazine is filled with articles about real young people attempting to understand their faith and put it into practice. The articles are well written, and kids can really identify with them because they touch real life. This is an excellent publication. Contact them at gp4t@guideposts.com or 39 Seminary Hill Road, Carmel, NY 10512.

Youth Bibles

Student's Life Application Bible. **Wheaton, IL: Tyndale House Publishers, 1997.**

The best youth Bible on the market today, this Bible comes in an easy-to-read text with helpful notes. The features include Moral Dilemma notes that utilize real-life situations and give biblical guidance to motivate right action; Megathemes that relate significant biblical themes to everyday life (with study questions); Ultimate Issue notes that address tough questions such as, Does God Exist; Here's What I Did notes that explain, through personal testimony, how individual students applied Scripture to difficult situations in their lives; Life Application notes that explain God's Word and help students apply it. Character sketches, charts, diagrams, time lines and overviews are also included.

Other excellent youth Bibles include *God's Word for Students* (World Publishing) and *Extreme Teen* (Thomas Nelson Publishers). Nelson also publishes a number of *Extreme Faith* books for teens.

Endnotes

Chapter One

1. Wayne Rice, *Junior High Ministry* (Grand Rapids, MI: Zondervan Publishing House, 1998), p. 34.
2. George Barna, *Third Millennium Teens* (Ventura, CA: The Barna Research Group, Ltd., 1999), p. 52.

Chapter Two

1. Susan Tifft, *Time* (June 26, 1989), p. 51.
2. Richard Gallagher, "Teenagers in Trouble: Understanding and Preventing Tragic Outcomes," *PBS Online*, 1999. http://www.pbs.org/wgbh/pages/frontline/shows/georgia/isolated/index.html (accessed May 31, 2000).
3. Grunwald Associates, "Children, Families, and the Internet 2000," *Grunwald Associates*, June 7, 2000. http://www.grunwald.com/survey/survey_content.html (accessed June 16, 2000).
4. Dr. Jim Geddes, *You Can Enjoy Your Teen* (Old Tapan, NJ: Fleming H. Revell, 1989), n.p.
5. Walt Mueller, *Understanding Today's Youth Culture* (Wheaton, IL: Tyndale House Publishers, 1999), pp. 16, 17.
6. Source unknown.
7. Mueller, *Understanding Today's Youth Culture*, pp. 225, 226.
8. Source unknown.
9. Source unknown.
10. Paula Rinehart, "Losing Our Promiscuity," *Christianity Today*, vol. 44, no. 8 (July 10, 2000), p. 34.
11. Source unknown.
12. Kay S. Hymowitz, *Ready or Not, Why Treating Children as Small Adults Endangers Their Future—and Ours* (New York: The Free Press, 1999), p. 164.
13. Janet Cool, "Nearing Adulthood, or: Why You'd Hate to be 13 Again," *Chicago Tribune*, January 24, 1989, n.p.

14. Hillary Rodham Clinton, "Parenting a Teen," *Newsweek*, May 8, 2000. http://www.newsweek.com.
15. Susan Tifft, *Time* (June 26, 1989), p.51.
16. Merton P. and A. Irene Strommen, *Five Cries of Parents* (San Francisco: Harper and Row, 1993), p. 68-73, 103.
17. Barna, *Third Millenium Teens*, p. 16.
18. Strommen, *Five Cries of Parents*, p. 82.
19. David Whitman, "The Youth Crisis," *usnews.com*, May 5, 1997. http://www.usnews.com/usnews/issue/970505/5chil.htm (accessed June 6, 2000).
20. Robert Bezilla, ed., *America's Youth in the 1990s* (Princeton, NJ: The George H. Gallup International Institute, 1993), n.p.

Chapter Three

1. Patricia Hersch, "A Tribe Apart: America's Teenagers," *Washingtonpost.com*. http://www.discuss.washingtonpost.com (accessed June 1, 2000).
2. Barna, *Third Millennium Teens*, p. 68.
3. Joe Bayly, "God's in the Toy Box," *Eternity Magazine* (January 1979), n.p.
4. Barna, *Third Millennium Teens*, p. 67.
5. Win and Charles Arn, "Closing the Evangelistic Back Door," *Leadership Journal* (spring 1984), n.p.
6. Bill Perkins and Dr. Rod Cooper, *Kids in Sports* (Portland, OR: Multnomah Press, 1989), p. 161.
7. Wayne Rice, "Every Kid Needs an Adult Friend," in *Parents and Children*, eds. Jay Kesler, Ron Beers and LaVonne Neff (Wheaton, IL: Victor Books, 1986), p. 388.
8. Dr. Bruce B. Barton and Dr. James C. Galvin, "Can We Take Modeling Too Far?" in *Parents and Teenagers*, eds. Jay Kesler and Ron Beers (Wheaton, IL: Victor Books, 1984), p. 65.

Chapter Four

1. Strommen, *Five Cries of Parents*, p. 69.

2. Barna, *Third Millennium Teens*, p. 18.
3. Gary Chapman, *The Five Love Languages of Teenagers* (Chicago: Northfield Publishing, 2000), p. 28.
4. Thomas Hime, *The Rise and Fall of the American Teenager* (New York: Avon Books, Inc., 1999), p. 282.
5. Dr. Cliff Schimmels, *When Junior Highs Invade Your Home* (Ada, MI: Baker Books, Fleming H. Revell Company, 1990), p. 115.
6. Dr. Ross Campbell, *How to Really Love Your Child* (Wheaton, IL: Victor Books, 1977), p. 18
7. Robert DeMoss, Jr., *Teen Tune-Up: A Parent's Primer on Popular Youth Culture* (Pomona, CA: Focus on the Family, 1989), n.p.
8. Nicki Reno, "Wow! WyldLife," *Inside Young Life*, vol. 7, no. 3 (June/July 2000), p. 2.

Chapter Five

1. *Newsweek* (July 10, 1989), n.p.
2. Marc Silver, "Is Volunteering a Waste of Time," *usnews.com*, April 28, 1997.
   http://www.usnews.com/usnews/issue/970428/28vob2.htm.
3. Scott Noon, "Shopping for Jr. High Volunteers," *Group's Junior High Ministry* (September/October 1989), n.p.

Chapter Six

1. Lydia I. Carlson, unpublished. Used by permission.
2. E. G. von Trutzschler, "Youth Ministry Is More Than a Meeting," in *The Youth Leader's Sourcebook*, ed. Gary Dausey (Grand Rapids, MI: Zondervan Publishing House, 1991), p. 41.
3. Dean Borgman, *When Kumbaya Is Not Enough: A Practical Theology for Youth Ministry* (Peabody, MA: Hendrickson Publishing, 1997), p. 113.
4. Mike Yaconelli, quoted in "The Bests, the Worsts, the Firsts," *Youthworker* (winter 1995), n.p.
5. Laura Lafoon and Dr. Carla Waterman, *Campus Life/JV Newsletter* (1988), n.p.

Chapter Seven

1. Wayne Rice, "Focus on Junior High," *Youthworker* (fall 1988), p. 17.
2. Bill Sanders, *Seize the Moment, Not Your Teen* (Wheaton, IL: Tyndale House Publishers, 1997), p. 101.
3. Dave Veerman, *Campus Life/JV Newsletter* (July 1986), n.p.
4. Greg Johnson, *Campus Life/JV Newsletter* (1986), n.p.
5. Jim Burns, *The Youth Builder* (Eugene, OR: Harvest House Publishers, 1988), p. 71.
6. Rice, *Junior High Ministry*, p. 33.

Chapter Eight

1. Rice, *Junior High Ministry*, p. 158.
2. Scott Noon, "Are You an Entertainer or a Minister?" *Group Magazine* (April/May 1989), n.p.
3. Sandy Jones, *Campus Life/JV Newsletter* (1986), n.p.
4. Greg Johnson, *Campus Life/JV Newsletter* (1986), n.p.
5. Rice, "Focus on Junior High," p. 18.
6. Johnson, *Campus Life/JV Newsletter*, n.p.

Chapter Nine

1. *Webster's New World College Dictionary*, 4th ed., s.v. "model," "role model," "value," "teach" and "skill."
2. Rice, "Focus on Junior High," p. 19.
3. H. Stephen Glenn and Jane Nelson, *Raising Self-Reliant Children in a Self-Indulgent World* (Rocklin, CA: Prima Publishing, 1989), p. 49.
4. Dr. Peter L. Benson, *Source*, n.d., n.p.
5. Dwight Spotts, *Campus Life/JV Newsletter* (1988), n.p.

Chapter Ten

1. Barna, *Third Millennium Teens*, p. 49.
2. Dave Veerman, *How to Apply the Bible* (Grand Rapids, MI: Baker Book House, 1999), p. 39.
3. Ajith Fernando, "Does God Speak Through the Bible?" in *Practical*

Christianity, ed. LaVonne Neff (Wheaton, IL: Tyndale House Publishers, 1987), p. 382.

4. Ronald T. Habermas, "How Should We Teach Biblical Truth," in *Reaching a Generation for Christ*, eds. Richard R. Dunn and Mark H. Senter III (Chicago: Moody Press, 1997), pp. 386-392.

5. Dave Veerman, "People, Plot, Point, Present, Plan," *Campus Life/JV— Year One* (1987), pp. 177-215.

Chapter Eleven

1. Les Christie, *How to Work with Rude, Obnoxious and Apathetic Kids* (Wheaton, IL: Victor Books, 1994), p. 9.

2. Chapman, *The Five Love Languages of Teenagers*, pp. 180, 181.

3. Borgman, *When Kumbaya Is Not Enough*, p. 170.

4. Wayne Stuart, *Campus Life/JV Newsletter*, n.d., n.p.

5. Nancy McGuirk, "Managing Unwanted Classroom Behavior," staff handout.

6. Wayne Rice, *Cleared for Takeoff* (Nashville, TN: Word Publishing, 2000), pp 132, 133.

7. Christie, *How to Work with Rude, Obnoxious and Apathetic Kids*, p. 112.